A

SCHOOL

FOR

PHOUJONG

A SCHOOL FOR PHOUJONG

ສະເພາະ ໂຮງຮຽນ ພູຈອງ

AN INTIMATE INSIGHT INTO VILLAGE
LIFE IN REMOTE NORTHERN LAOS

Trish Clark

"I have been / am haunted by the grim and momentous developments in the Middle-East, Africa and Europe and to learn of such a thoroughly positive event such as your school is like seeing a beacon in the gloom!"

Helga Fiedler-Boehme

ARCHAEOLOGIST / HISTORIAN

Designed in Australia and published
by
High Adventure Publishing.com
Tumbulgum, 2490 Australia
© Trish Clark 2016
ISBN10   0-9807848-9-1
ISBN13   978-0-9807848-9-3

Cover design :   Iain Finlay

Photographs :   Iain Finlay and Trish Clark

KOPCHAI LAI-LAI
to

Lisa Parnell, *Alan Wilson* and *Trevor McCosker*, who have hung in there since the very beginning.

...to every single one of you who has supported our Laos Projects...

and of course the inestimable *Chanthy Sisombuth*.

Along with all respect and gratitude to every villager in Phoujong and NaLin for your graceful open-heartedness and the fearless manner in which you welcomed two strangers into your lives.

But as always my most heartfelt thanks to *Iain*, who has turned each day of the last fifty-plus years we have spent together into a great adventure.

CONTENTS

Phoujong and NaLin villages.. showing road and river access from former royal capital Luang Prabang

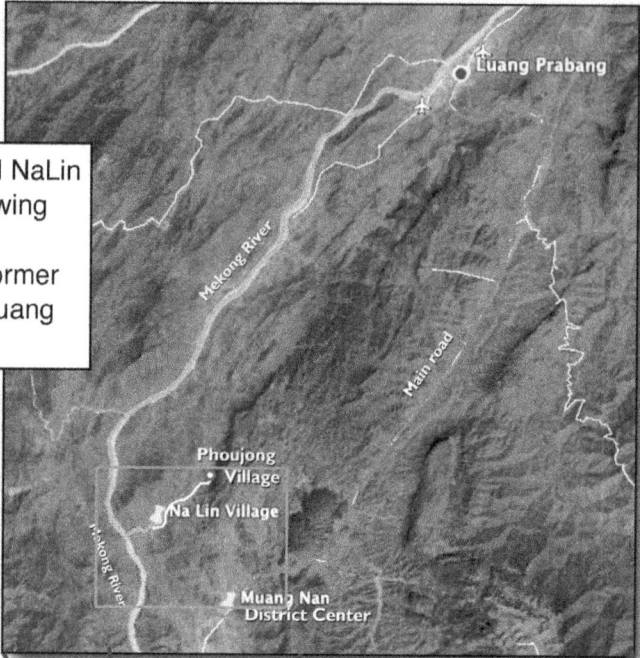

Phoujong and NaLin location in northern Laos

Rough road leading inland from the river to NaLin and Phoujong villages.

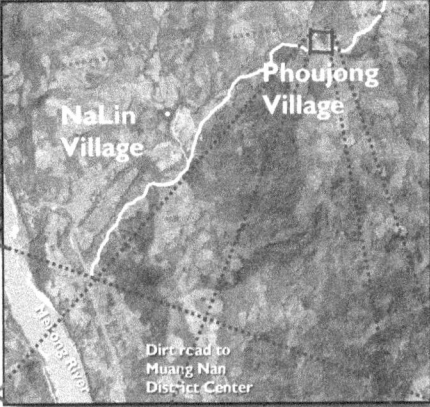

A satellite view of Phoujong Village shows sun reflecting off the roof of the new school.

1 INTO THE UNKNOWN

Its one thing to make a leap into the unknown, quite another to do so while freighted to the gills with the high expectations and funds of others.

But it had to be done. A School for Phoujong needed to be built before the annual torrential rains came, or we would lose not only a year of building opportunity but, with it the confidence of the Project's financial supporters. So it had to be done now.

We realized that the friends we had made through fund-raising were sure that we knew what we were doing. They refused to allow us to disabuse them of this falsity. They wanted to believe in us. No one wanted to hear that building a school was an unknown step for us and came with a new set of parameters. We had managed to earn their trust and they didn't want us to express any doubts or even any anxieties. We simply couldn't let them down. We could not fail them.

So we sent the hard-earned A$28,000 from the Project's bank account at Murwillumbah, in northern New South Wales, to Chanthy Sisombuth's personal bank account in Luang Prabang, the former Royal Capital of the People's Democratic Republic of Laos. In the process we lost A$7000. That's how far the Australian dollar had plummeted over the previous few months against the US dollar in a seemingly never-ending slide. Heartrending.

Then we went for our daily swim in the magically calming waters of our nearby ocean creek. And there it happened again; the see-saw of experiences and emotions that we had almost come to expect since starting on this journey five years before.

A woman we knew detached herself from the group she was swimming with and coming up alongside me asked, 'when are you going to Laos again?' 'The day after tomorrow,' I told her. Vicki looked alarmed and began stroking back towards the beach of the little cove while calling over her shoulder, 'that's great. I will call my friend immediately. Her ninety-one year old mother has made thirty-three dresses for little girls that she wants you to take up.'

'Please don't tell Iain, not right now,' I managed to shout to her as she went up the sand and began rummaging in her beach-bag for her mobile phone.

'Tell me what?' Iain asked, emerging from the water beside me.

'Oh, nothing.' I took a deep breath but realizing it was impossible to dissemble further, added 'and I can take care of it all.'

'What all?' He was grumpy and not just because of the depredations on the Project's funds. This morning we had woken to find the plastic plumbing running under the kitchen deck outside our rural home had sprung a leak; small but not something that would cure itself. He would have to slither into the less than one metre high, dark earthen space and hopefully repair it.

I gave a nervously garbled account of the thirty-three dresses that had suddenly become an addition to our already packed and weighed luggage for Laos. Right then Vicki came back down the sand, phone in hand, and with a broad smile assured us that to save us any additional bother her friend would bring her all-but-centenarian mother plus the dresses to our place that very afternoon.

It turned into an occasion to remember and a terrific antidote to the financial loss of the morning. Though all Iain remembers is many hours of scrummaging in the oozing squelch in thirty-degree - plus heat and the frustrations of searching through his handyman's plumbing stores trying various sized pieces of piping and fixtures before finally solving the problem.

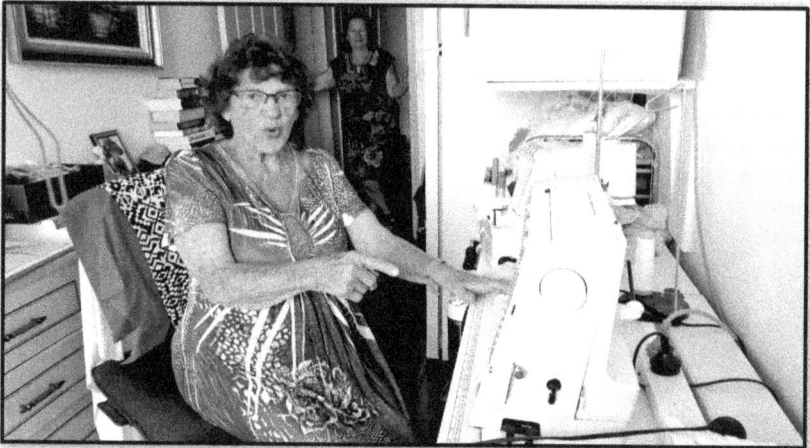

Ms Babette at her sewing machine

Meanwhile Babette, for that was the elderly seamstress's elegant name, and her daughter Barbara and her grand-daughter Justine and I oohed and aahed over the perfect little dresses smelling so freshly of crisp new cotton. Each was adorned with Babette's nametag. We took photographs and exchanged stories and drank copious amounts of tea while folding and re-folding the designer pieces to make them as small and manageable as possible before squeezing them into two vacuum-sealed storage bags and vacuuming the air out of them. The result weighed under a kilo each.

I tried explaining to the ladies how much they would be appreciated by girls who would never before have received such a beautiful new cotton dress. But I realized that whatever words I used, I would fail. It was just the first step again across the inevitable divide that opens up when we leave here and go there. It is impossible to bridge this with mere words. All I could say was, Thank you. Thank you. Kopchai. Kopchai, for such a gift from the heart.

**

For Iain and I our whole experience in Laos has been a serendipitous gift from the heart: almost always unanticipated and challenging but inevitably deeply enriching as well as good fun.

It began in 2010 when we chose to cut ourselves off physically from anyone we knew and in that much needed solitude to hunker down in Luang Prabang and work fulltime at our own various writing projects.

We developed a friendship with a young Lao lad, nineteen-year-old Chanthy Sisombuth, who was supporting his studies at an English Language College by working as a waiter in one of the myriad riverside restaurants.

We started by helping him with his English and then his college fees and then, after some months, with the rent for a small room. Every day he would visit us in the guesthouse where we had taken a long-term rental on a room with the all-important prerequisite of a workspace with a view of great beauty from its big balcony. Here we would chat in English with Chanthy as well as doing some very basic language tuition.

He was bright, personable, determined, and always on time. Right from the start we enjoyed each other's company. Naturally he told his parents about all this, explaining to us that they were poor rice farmers. When the time came for us to resume the mixed blessings of family life and home-ownership in Australia, in a heart-gesture of thanks for assisting their son, they invited us to visit them.

Looking back everything that has happened in our lives since that occasion has been an unplanned but natural progression.

The Sisombuth's village, NaLin, is close to three hours south of Luang Prabang, by either a boat on the Mekong or by local bus along Route 12. As with everything in Lao, the timeframe is only ever an estimate as it is dependent on road and river conditions as well as the inevitable unplanned-for events.

Going by bus to Sayaboury you ask to be put off in the District Centre of Muang Nan and from there you need to cadge a paid-for lift from someone who happens to be travelling, invariably in a far from comfortable clapped-out farm vehicle, up into the valley of the Hadsaik River that meanders down from the rounded, jungled summit of Phoujong Mountain. Phoujong translates as rice ladle, which is what the silhouette of the mountain somewhat resembles.

If you go by boat you need to arrange to be landed, as near as conditions allow, at Hadsaikam and from there the same casual hired transport applies, but is more difficult to find.

You don't want to be doing this with a schedule to meet, because you won't.

On that first visit we were treated to a traditional baci ceremony and welcomed into the family. Chanthy's Dad we discovered, was the *naiban* or Village Headman, so through him we met with other villagers. When we left we knew that we couldn't just walk away and do nothing. The village of around 250 people had no running water, no electricity, no school and the nearest medical help was several hours walk away. But pivotal to all this was that what linked these people to the outside world was a rough track that in the wet season turned into a knee-deep quagmire of barely negotiable mud. This road, we felt, was the initial key to breaking the nexus of isolation.

So in a mad rush of blood to the head we returned to Australia, sure that we could raise sufficient funds, $50 thousand dollars we originally estimated, to build The Road to NaLin.

The process took longer and was far more frustrating as well as educational than we had naively imagined but we did it. (You can read about it in *The Road to NaLin*)

A year later, after struggling to raise more funds at home, we went back and put in sixteen sorely required culvert drains to assist with diverting and draining the destructively heavy annual rains. It was during this time that we went further up the Hadsaik River Valley to watch the digging-in of the biggest and most needed of the culverts that went through the village of Phoujong. Here we saw that the need was far greater even than in NaLin. The 300 or so villagers, were members of the acutely disadvantaged minority group, the Hmong and, we were later to discover, the most crushed of all, the Yao Mien.

As with NaLin there was no running water to the simple houses almost all of which have dirt floors and thatched rooves. No electricity. The nearest medical facilities were more than an hour away over an unmade road but at least there was a school, or so we had been told.

We had travelled up in a 4 wheel-drive kindly loaned for the day by a Government Department, crammed in with Chantha, a woman from the National Library and three of her assistants. Bringing eagerly sought-after books, as well as clothing for the three score Primary School pupils aged five to twelve, the quartet also organized simple singing games. After an initial wariness the children got into the spirit of the visit, though their parents remained watching from a careful distance.

Ferynin with the first book of her own

Lowhin and his friends are fascinated by Lao fairy tales

We also met the sole teacher, Kaojien Zaethan and when we asked if we could see his school he led us down into a gully on the far edge of the settlement. We clambered up the other side and there it was. Surrounded by an area of raw dirt, collapsing in on itself: a one-room dilapidated tin-roofed shack with a baked dry earthen floor that had wide cracks opened by the staggering heat.

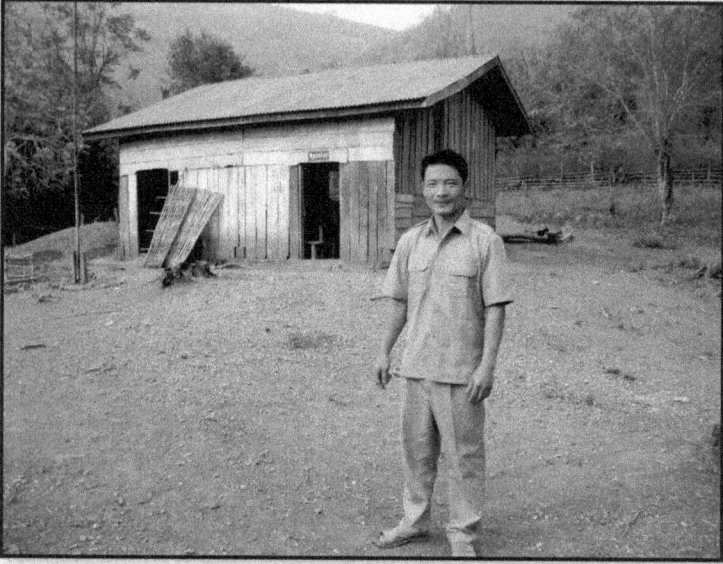

Sole teacher Kaojien and his original school house

There were a few battered benches and tables, a blackboard and in some desultory attempt to give the place an aura of learning, vividly coloured charts of the human body had been attached to the woven split bamboo walls. That was it.

Listening to Kaojien, via Chanthy's translation, talk about his thirty-five students we had one of those light-bulb moments when everything becomes so clear you cannot fail to understand. To break the chain it is invariably necessary to start at the beginning: here that meant at the literal ground floor.

These children, the next generation of Lao, required being encouraged into believing in themselves; their value as human beings and their full potential. Knowing that someone else believes in you is the start of all that. So we decided to try to build them a School.

A School for Phoujong.

2 THE ADVENTURE BEGINS

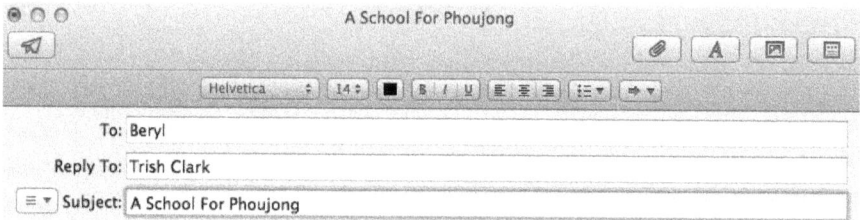

● ○ ○   A School For Phoujong

⟨✈⟩   ⟨📎⟩ ⟨A⟩ ⟨🖼⟩ ⟨▦⟩

              Helvetica ⬍ 14⬍ ■ B I U ≣ ≣ ≣ ⁚≡▾ ⇨▾

        To: Beryl

  Reply To: Trish Clark

≣▾ Subject: A School For Phoujong

Sabaidee Beryl!

Hope you are staying healthy...happy...and knitting up a storm!

Meanwhile...the adventure here has begun!

Iain has had fun with his compass and tape-measure. We have signed up Mr. Khong as the Builder. Thongkhanh, (Chanthy's father) as Site Supervisor and Chanthy as Mr. Fixer, Translator and General Hold-It-All-Together-Chap. All of them are delighted!!!! The financial spillover effect into not only their lives but into the general community will be much appreciated.

I already have plans involving the women of Phoujong with their splendiferous embroidery!!

The land has been cleared; first by hand by the Phoujong villagers, then by Mr.Pham from Nan Nouan, with his tractor/rotary-hoe.

The Education Dept. has had its two-bobs worth of input by increasing the size of the teacher's room by 40cms! And we have all signed the papers. Even the District Governor is all set to go. But Chinese New Year has shut down all government offices! for four days!!

The Phoujong villagers are also all fired up to go into the forest to chop timber for formwork but a Lao Loum wedding and a Yao spirit festival has put a hold on this for two day. So we came back up to LPB for a shower/food intake (apologies but raw pig's liver and raw buffalo are a bridge too far for me! Tho I do a good pretence!)

Also to be in touch with family and friends and to catch up with the 'other world' of Australia etc.

I haven't told you about the 33 dresses made by 91 year-old Babette Scott from Banora Point, Queensland...that were donated to us the day before we left! and that we brought up and gave to the teachers to hand out to their pupils. Of course there were not enough for everyone, but the happiness in other student's happiness and the warm sharing with the boys, who of course missed out, was so splendid to see. First time for new fresh-smelling *crisp cotton beautiful dresses. The world needs more Babettes.*

Thank you/Kopchai for being a BIG part of this. We will keep you up to speed as things progress.

BIG hugs...t/i

I have decided to include some of my emails in this story because they capture the moment as well as my intense joy. To give you a clue: the number of exclamation marks is a significant indicator on the happiness index!

The adventure had indeed begun. We had spent a couple of days reacquainting ourselves with our friends in the village of NaLin. This meant sleeping on floor-mats in the Sisombuth family house, something that has become increasingly difficult; for Iain because his aging prostate demands several visits to the outside loo during the night and for me because my knees had deteriorated to the point where they both require a total replacement and not even in the comfort of my own bed at home am I now able to get an uninterrupted night's pain-free rest. I tell you about these personal physical frailties so that you get the real picture not some Gauguin idealization of living a simple village life. There is nothing, absolutely nothing, glamorous or enviable about poverty.

Mr. Pham drives Iain around on his tractor

In the year since our last visit much had changed.

Frail Mr. Pho Simaneevong, the septugenarian relative of Chanthy's mother had died. He had spent his life as a fisherman on the mighty Mekong but when he was no longer able to care for himself or for his same-aged wife, she had gone to live with relatives near Vientiane and he to live in a curtained-off partition at one end of the Sisombuth's family room. Now his former living space has become storage for hessian bags holding the year's vital rice supplies for the entire extended family.

As one life had ended another had began.

Chanthy's sister Bounlee, younger than her brother by three years, had completed her training at the Teacher's College in Luang Prabang, established a job for herself at the NaLin Primary School, married fellow-teacher Mr. Kone and they now had a three month old baby son, Jarrah.

People mostly don't shilly-shally about with such decisions in Laos. The shortness of life expectancy, 63 for women and 59 for men, leaves little time for umming and aahing.

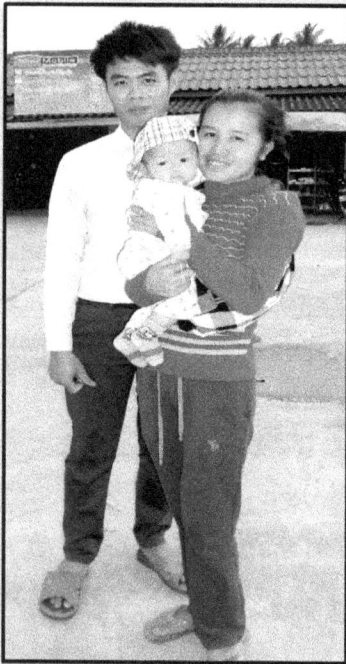

Bounlee and Kone with Jarrah

We had been asked to choose their son's name and we felt a strong, hardwood tree, straight of limb with deep roots, was a good totem. So he became Jarrah.

In Lao culture the man takes up residence with his wife's family. Mr. Kone had built a brick partition that reached slightly above head height at the far end of the Sisombuth's main room and this was now a private area for the little family.

During the nights I could hear baby Jarrah fidgeting around for his mother's breast. I could smell the stored garlic heads hanging from the rafters above us and the earthy aroma coming from the stacked bags of sticky rice. Around 4.30am the distant crowing of cockerels set the near neighbour's roosters going. Before long Chanthy's mother, Buachanh is busying herself in the family cooking area while his father, Thongkhanh has lit a small outside fire nearby on the ground beside the washing area. Please do not ask me why I felt so deeply content because I could not find the words to explain.

Thongkhanh and Buachanh's other son is Jai who is a couple of years older than Chanthy. He had also made large-scale life changes while we had been away. Already married to Binh and now with an almost two year old son Sydney (not difficult to guess who also named him) Jai had at first followed the Lao custom of living with his wife's family, on the edge of the District Centre of Muang Nan.

He had worked his in-law's small rice-holding as well as the Sisombuth family's rice field and somehow managed to also branch out on his own, on leased land, where he had planted hops. It was a heavy load even for a man of his obvious physical strength and determination to get ahead.

For whatever reasons, we didn't pry, but it was slowly let drop, matters did not work out so well with his in-laws, so Jai and Binh and Sydney had moved back to the village of NaLin where they were in the process of creating their own lifestyle. This involved them building their own house that was decidedly simpler than any of the other houses in the village. Tacked together from bits and bobs of left-over timber it was a L'il Abner style home surrounded by a wonky fence which gave it the air of a frail fortress.

Jai is touchingly proud of this construction inside which he has planted a veggie garden and penned his great pride, three large black pigs. We had talked over this possibility the last time we had stayed and it gives us a big charge to see the way he has run with the scheme. We had read up a little on pig rearing and found that for all that they are hefty beasts and seemingly strong a pig's constitution is surprisingly (to an ignorant person like me) vulnerable. For the first few months of life piglets need to be kept warm and fed nutritious food while at the same time protected from their mother who can so easily roll over and squash the life out of them. As they mature, if you want a sow to be a good breeder and the male to put on heft so as to fetch a good sales price for his meat, they need to be well fed. This is not going to happen if they are simply left to roam about the village scrounging for scraps especially in communities where what you might think of as scraps can be turned into a family meal. Jai's pigs were being well fed and just as essential in this heat, kept hosed down and watered. They had also been given the all-important immunization shots to keep them healthy. Along with all this Jai is still working his hops. He and Binh have plans to have Sydney well educated and they know this will cost money.

Meantime Binh is creating her own niche market in Lao-lao, the brain-zappingly potent rice wine that is a total necessity at *baci* ceremonies and a staple relaxant and hunger suppressant in the country's harsh rural life. More recently it has even found its way into the bars and restaurants of the cities, though here it is usually spiced up and even coloured to make it more amenable to western palates and eyes.

Over the coming weeks we purchase a horde of five-gallon plastic containers from the bottled water factory in LPB and bring them down on the bus. Thus we become part of their production unit: helping to create pig meat we never eat and Lao-lao that Iain alone drinks and then only when totally compelled to by peer group pressure during baci ceremonies.

We watch, along with Sydney, as Binh steams the rice and stores the resultant liquid. Later we are invited to the ceremonial pouring of the first batch of her Lao-lao into the containers on the outsides of which she marks the level, alongside the date of the bottling, just as carefully as if it had been a cask of fine wine.

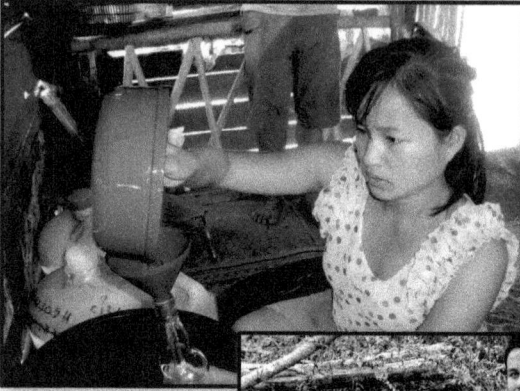

Binh bottling her Lao-lao rice wine

Jai making Lao-lao deliveries

While she works, carefully scrutinized by Sydney who even generously offers us a tasting, we come up with suggestions for names that could be stuck on these bottles as part of a marketing campaign. Not that Lao-lao needs additional marketing. It markets itself by word of mouth. Their plan is for Jai to take phone orders from around the district and make deliveries by motorbike.

It is easy to imagine Sydney, in his later years, boasting to impressed youngsters, 'my Mother made the best illegal hooch in Laos'.

The age-old aphorism that the apple doesn't fall

far from the tree, or in this instance, perhaps more accurately, one rice grain doesn't grow far from the last, is mightily apparent in the Sisombuth family. They are a close-knit, tight unit of similarities.

Father Thongkhanh's wiry and determined strength is shot through with a gleamingly apparent honesty and integrity while despite her physically tiny frame Mother Bouchanh is without doubt the determined glue that gives the necessary day-to-day strength to the family unit.

It is because of this shared quality leadership that the Sisombuth family, in the face of what most *falang* would see as overwhelming odds, are in the position of having several bases covered:

One son, Jai, is still working land he owns. This means that if push comes to shove, as it so often does in this part of the world, one of the siblings will know how to grow enough food to feed everyone at least at subsistence level; so no one will starve.

A daughter, Bounlee, who as a teacher brought a sizeable bride price, is now a Government employee. This means some degree of social status and security even though teachers and other professionals employed by the Government, such as nurses, are frequently not paid for months at a time. There is some hope that as Laos claws it way up the economic ladder this will happen less often.

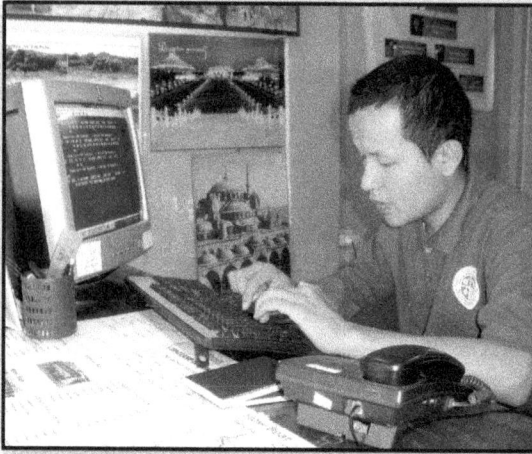

Chanthy at work in the travel bureau office

And their other son, Chanthy, who by completing his English Language course and now studying Business Administration in LPB, as well as having a full time job in the tourist industry, has broken the mould of tradition by leaving his home village. By learning a foreign language he has become a part of the growing consumer society and a wider world. He is the foot in the door to the future.

Of course, none of this is one-hundred-percent proof against natural disasters such as flooding rains or personal accidents that lurk menacingly in every unguarded parang or newly formed pothole. Sydney has already had a broken leg when a tempting motorbike upped and fell over on him.

Nor is it a certainty against the results of selfish greed in other parts of the world. But by working as a unit they have managed to lengthen the on-the-ground omnipresent poor odds.

We were especially glad in NaLin to meet up with Thongdy Thongsamou who, being a couple of years even older than Iain, has come to be extra-special to us. Despite having no shared language the two of them have developed an empathy and pleasure in other's company. Like a couple of old roosters they compare failing

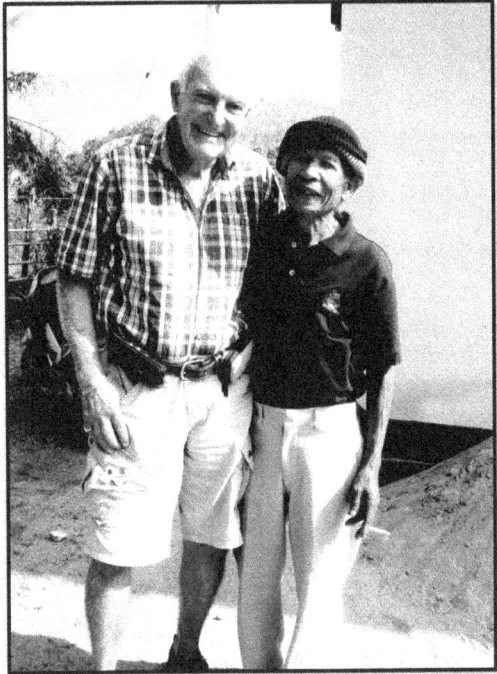

Thongdy and Iain. Two elderly roosters

muscle tone and joke about the joys of having younger (even if only by a few years) wife who keep them neat, tidy and somewhat in check

But despite our feeling so at home in NaLin we quickly come to realise we couldn't... or more strongly than that... we shouldn't, stay in the village. NaLin is a settlement of the country's majority Lao Loum people. Phoujong is home to minority people. It would be counter-productive to settle in with our pals in NaLin while the school in Phoujong was being built. It would be seen as something almost akin to sleeping with the enemy. The slight, but still palpable, uneasiness of the social relationship between these groups of people was something we, in our *falang* ignorance, had not taken much account of but we very soon grasped that if we were to be accepted it had to be on Phoujong's terms.

So we decide to use a modest guesthouse in Muang Nan, some 18 kms away, as our local base, having already accepted that we would also need to spend restorative hits of time in LPB. All of these realizations and decisions were not pre-planned but simply fell into place and were made on the very first day we visited the building site.

Almost from the moment our plane touched down in LPB we had been made constantly aware that the window of time in which to build A School for Phoujong was finite and governed by the fickle annual rains. So it was frustrating that it had taken the first week to negotiate by mobile phone through a longwinded chain of communication; first through Chanthy to Phoujong Headman, Laisiew and then to the village of Nan Nuan which is more than twenty kilometres of boulder strewn rough track further up into the mountains. Nan Nuan is also a village of minority people and here lived a Mr. Pham, who had sent a translated letter, photograph attached, to us in Australia some months previously suggesting the use of his tractor and rotary hoe combination for the necessary land-clearing.

We'd had a scare when a few days before we left home an email had arrived from Chanthy saying that Headman Laisiew would like the new school built in an area shown, also in attached photographs, as being steep and thickly forested. We'd emailed by return saying that clearing and flattening such land was way beyond our budget. The idea was never mentioned again. But we got the distinct feeling that matters needed to be thrashed out between Laisiew and Mr. Pham plus others and that was why the delay.

Over the coming weeks there would be quite an amount of this sensation of fumbling and stumbling through clouds of unknowingness. Though we become somewhat canny at managing many times to turn this to our advantage

**

The noise made by Mr. Pham's mechanical combo shatters the valley's silence. Brimful with confidence the village's young boys, who have been enjoying a weekend game of soccer, race up and down beside him at the edge of the growing clearing.

Teacher Kaojien comes to greet us with his warm smile. Mr. Pham had started at daybreak and by the time we'd got a lift up the track from Muang Nan he was well in to the process of flattening a big area behind the present shack of a school. The previous day the men of Phoujong had taken time out from the constant demands of their farms to roughly clear the land of shrubs and a few sizeable surface tree logs.

There are still a number of massive tree roots to wrestle up from deep in the soil and while Iain immediately clambers onboard the big red tractor to film some action, the air fills with the sensuous smell of freshly turned earth.

More hesitantly the young village girls come up the hill, hanging together in a protective group, to sit on a fallen tree stump and watch the fun

Mr. Khong Khousanvath, Bounlee's father-in-law, is already on-site. We had met him the previous year when he had transformed the dark hole in the Sisombuth's family home that Buachanh used as her kitchen. Squatting on her haunches over a fire lit on bricks set on the mud floor, beating and pounding, steaming and frying she kept up with the constant demands of feeding an expanding family of agricultural workers.

With a small amount of the funds left over from putting in sixteen culvert drains we had set up a simple trial system bringing water into the house from six large plastic bins set on a raised platform built along one exterior wall of the home.

Mr. Khong had built a kitchen bench that sported

a metal sink and a tap, as well as tiling the floor of both the cooking area and the main room. We knew even from this slight acquaintance that he was a hard worker plus that he had building skills.

Over the past few months he had also built a proper room for the Sisombuth family's ablutions so that instead of dangerously slipping and sliding on the uneven moldy pavers under the outdoor standpipe there was now a slosh-over bathing room and as part of that, a squat dunny with a door. He had a vested interest in getting this job done because he was quite apparently very fond of his first grandchild, Jarrah, whose name he told us he liked a lot, even more so when we told him of its tree roots in Western Australia.

We hadn't inquired about any further building experience. In Lao, we had come to realize you go with the flow. So it was yet another example of serendipity when as the weeks went by we learnt that Mr. Khong had plenty of professional experience. He had built houses in the capital, Vientiane. He had even built schools with aid money from the Koreans. Fact is we accepted him because Thongkhanh vouched for him, not in so many words, but simply by choosing him and we had developed a total trust in Thongkhanh who is also waiting on-site.

Iain has brought with him from home a setsquare and an expanding tape-measure. In LPB's Chinese

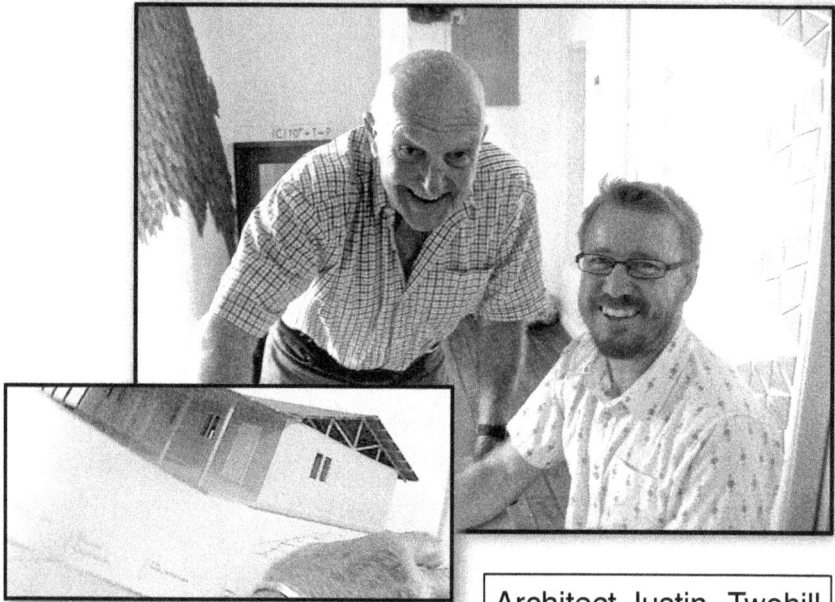

Architect Justin Twohill and his school plans

market we had purchased a compass.

But what really gets everyone excited is the roll of architect's plans. Friend and Murwillumbah resident, architect Justin Twohill had drawn these up, graciously gratis.

There had been a couple of touching blips in design suggestions as for instance when Justin had included an outdoor shoe-storage rack. Quite understandable, unless you have witnessed the unconscious ease with which everyone in Laos, toddlers to aged folk, step without breaking stride out of their sandals before entering any room, leaving a huddle of plastic flip flops by the door to be slipped back into, like extensions to the body, on departure.

We had all mulled over the idea that we build a two-room schoolhouse using a sliding divider wall. 'So it can convert into a big multi-function building that can be used by the whole community, perhaps for meetings after work or at weekends.' Sounded good when sitting in Justin's office and we agreed that schoolrooms are often a wasted resource in Australia, laying empty for a good chunk of the year.

But when we present this idea to Kaojien he dismisses it without pause and when later we heard the loud chanting of rote learning we couldn't but agree. A concrete-block dividing wall would keep the two rooms at least somewhat soundproof. Added to which Kaojien assures us, through Chanthy, 'the sliding mechanism would jam up with mud brought in from outside in the wet and the door mechanisms would quickly be broken by active young boys.' Kaojien was nothing if not practical and having been the teacher in a single-teacher school for twelve years we took all his advice on board.

We had also arrived burdened down with a political correctness that Kaojien also quickly crushed. In response to our wanting to know if there was a particular direction the School should face, perhaps to appease the Spirits, he dismisses the suggestion out of hand. 'Just build the school,' he instructs.

Well, if it was all about mere practicality what about angling the building to get the least of the strong summer sun and the most of the winter sun and were there any prevailing winds to take into account? Kaojien was adamant. 'Just build the school,' he reiterates with a smile that suggests he thinks we might be prevaricating and that his longed-for new building might slip through his fingers like some *falang* chimera.

Chanthy's father Thongkhanh, Teacher Kaojien, Iain and Chanthy discuss the siting of the school

Mr. Pham is paid off from the brick-sized wad of Lao kip banknotes Iain has already taken to carrying about in his daypack and a receipt is given. Mr. Khong, now designated Builder and Thongkhanh, now transformed into Building Site Supervisor alongside Mr. Fixit Chanthy, accompanied by Teacher Kaojien stride about in the heat on the leveled site with Iain waving his arms, the tape-measure and the architectural plans that gave him the vital look of knowing what he is doing. In this manner A School for Phoujong is marked out with string held in place by slivers of bamboo cut on the go from the surrounding forest whilst a horde of schoolboys follows and watches with interest.

Then we all, including the schoolboys, crouch in the small area of shade thrown by the present schoolhouse and Justin's plans are consulted and reconfigured. Kaojien wants an extra door into each room. This means windows will need to be rearranged. Iain says he will redraw the plans with the changed measurements concisely marked.

It is suddenly announced that tomorrow we will attend a meeting with the Head of the District Education Department that has been organized by Thongkhanh who knows somebody who has a relative in the Department. With no prior warning it is said that contracts will be drawn up and signed at this meeting.

We then learn that after tomorrow Phoujong village will be strictly off-limits to outsiders due to a two-day spirit ceremony and the day after that Mr. Khong's second daughter is getting married so it is arranged that building work will commence in three day's time.

It feels as though matters are suddenly moving very fast.

3 CONTRACTS

What to say about education in Laos other than it is the pits. Well not quite. There are a few countries where it is even worse. But when you are 137th out of the 153 listed on the World Index of Education there is only one way to aim and that's up

It is not that education is a low priority for the government of Laos. It is just that it can unfortunately be dismissed as an almost luxury in a country that is so poor there is very little to spend except on essentials... like hopefully ways of ensuring people don't actually starve. More than a quarter of the population survives way below the poverty level at a point where poor nutrition and actual malnutrition are a constant in life.

Laos is dependent on foreign aid for everything but the most basic human requirements. And as we all know the foreign aid budget in almost every donor country, most pertinently for us, Australia, is being continually slashed. Since we began our involvement with Laos, Australian Aid has dropped to an all-time low of 22cents in every $100 of National Income. A sobering statistic for people who imagine themselves to be citizens of a generous nation

The time for sharing seems to be, not just now thanks.

Laos's geography, history, and population size are multipliers of every downside. Mountainous, with only 5% of its terrain being cultivable, tiny and landlocked between expansionist neighbours; a former much neglected colony with a elitist monarchial system that was finally ousted by Communism and with only six and a half million people to get and keep the ball rolling, it is all too easy to delegate it to the too hard basket especially because it seemingly purposely keeps a very low profile and makes very few demands of the world community.

That's all the bad news for today. Perhaps a slow drip-feed of these downsides is the better way to go.

So, the miracle is that with 2.8% of the country's tiny GDP going towards education the overall literacy rate is presently 83% for men and 63% for women and more importantly, rising.

The French colonial administration, under which

the Vietnamese, another French colonial people, ran the Laos civil service, finally handed over power to the local population in the late fifties. This followed the ignominious defeat of the French Army by the Vietnamese, under the revered General Giap, at Dien Bien Phu.

Up to that time education was almost totally the preserve of the Buddhist *wats* where it was religion-based and conducted partially in Lao though also in the ancient Indian 'dead' language of Pali. Young boys...no girls...received very simple educational skills. Only those novices who stayed on to become ordained as monks benefitted from further studies.

It was not until the late 1960s that a basic Lao curriculum was even put on the Government's agenda. By the seventies still only 36% of school-age children were attending classes and it was not until the Communists took political power in 1984, in what is always referred to euphemistically as, The Change of Government, that the concept of Barefoot Teachers, already such a proven success in fellow-Communist neighbour China, was instituted, most valuably in regional areas and remote rural villages. It is estimated that this program reached 750 thousand adults.

Problems arose due to the lack of basic teaching materials such as books, paper and writing implements and without follow-through and practice a number of the people who had been reached in this manner lost these skills. But even in the face of these setbacks the literacy level reached 44%.

In 1986 the decentralization of the overall economy was begun and by 1988 63% of all school-age children were enrolled.

This general trend upward has continued though it is unfortunately often a case of two steps forward one step back as the date for the goal of a proposed universal primary education continues to be pushed onto a distant horizon.

Too many young children cannot reach even the low standards set and repeat their classes so that they may take double the years to complete a five year course. In remote rural areas there is also always family pressures for their labour on the farm. It is no surprise that too many children, more especially as you would anticipate, the girls, drop out of the education system and become agricultural labourers.

From tales told as our close friendship with Chanthy, developed over five years, we knew what total determination is needed to get through Primary and then to move on and complete Secondary schooling.

When we first met him Chanthy's stories of how he got through these years were always leavened with warmth and humour. In fact without the resilience that a sense of humour brings it would to my mind be all but impossible to get through what he endured.

What remains of Chanthy's old Primary School in NaLin Village

It was only bit-by-bit that we came to know the darker side of his experiences. This understanding only enhanced our admiration of his humanity and determined spirit.

Then there are the extra problems faced by would-be students from any of the at least forty-nine ethnic groups in Laos and who therefore come from a background in which Lao is only their second language as well as from a very different culture as almost all of them are also non-Buddhist.

This was the minefield into which we were innocently walking that already warm morning when we shook hands with a couple of genially welcoming Education Department officials at their simple office alongside the Muang Nan District Secondary School.

There had been no prior contact with anyone from the Education Department and to be honest we were prepared for there to be some form of required kickback. We'd heard such horror stories from people both in and out of country, *falangs* yes, but with experience in trying to get aid projects underway in Laos, that it seemed inevitable. We had even talked this through in advance and agreed that we would not pay any form of bribe to anyone at whatever level.

We had not done so when we built the Road to NaLin nor when we had installed the culverts. Even so we realized this was somewhat different.

If someone came into your community in Australia, a Chinese perhaps or, oops, a Pakistani and wanted to build a school where young minds would be trained, even though offering to do so for free, wouldn't you be asking questions and perhaps even looking for ways to turn it to personal advantage?

So with this underlying anxiety we were nervously on guard as we met Mr. Buanthone Sutiphone and Mr. Bounphong Vunasouk who looked pretty smart in their khaki-coloured uniforms with red shoulder tabs to denote rank. We have learnt to accept that this somewhat martial display is simply a cultural difference, though I still initially find it startling to see teachers dressed in military style. No more startling I tell myself than the seemingly next to naked bodies of young *falang* travellers must appear to the majority of Lao people.

There is quite a turnout crowded into the small office space and more chairs need to be brought from other rooms. From NaLin there is Headman Mr. Dith, Site-Supervisor Thongkhanh, Chanthy. Builder Khong comes from a village we have not yet visited, Namphai and then there's us.

From Phoujong there's Headman Laisiew and his Deputy Kaoseng along with Teacher Kaojien. There are also three faces we don't recognize; we are introduced to a man in his forties whose facial resemblance to Deputy Kaoseng is so strong they were obviously related and who we were told later was in fact his father. We soon came to realise he held quite a degree of power in the community. There is an elderly wizen-faced chap and another with a saturnine look tinged with a permanent dark scowl. The older man we would begin to see regularly in the village, often smoking a large water-cooled tobacco pipe. We came to understand that he was in some important way an integral part of the spiritual life of Phoujong. The scowler is introduced as Sanfin. Iain and I both sense he is a man to watch out for.

Pleasantries are exchanged. Light fragrant tea is sipped. There is an atmosphere of expectation. Convivial chatter subsides. Chair legs scrape harshly on the tiled floor. The Phoujongers, whom I now see are all sitting close together, separate from the Naliners, talk among themselves.

'What are they saying?' I ask Chanthy, who looks uncomfortable. 'I don't know.' He even sounds somewhat cross and for the first time we realize that though they all speak Lao, the people from Phoujong also speak a language that is unintelligible to outsiders.

Only Thongkhanh remains looking totally calm and at ease. There is, we realize not for the first time, something exceptional about this man. Nothing fazes him.

The door that has been slightly ajar opens wider to allow entry for an unusually tall Lao woman who exudes an air of style as well as professional confidence.

Iain and I recognize her immediately as someone we had met more than a year or so previously. We'd been guests at a dinner held to celebrate the completion of The Road and the

Madam Phoungkham Phensavath, Head of the Education Department for Nan District.

installation of the culverts. The Governor of Nan District attended together with a number of other local government officials.

Actually what we remember most about that evening is Chanthy consuming, with apparent relish, a sizeable amount of the buffalo that had been slaughtered to honour the festivities, along with the special delicacy of the buffalo's ears. Later that night and all the following day he had been violently sick.

I recall that this confident attractive woman had been at that dinner and also that she was with the Education Department because I could recall her mentioning at the time how very much they needed assistance. Here she was again, quite apparently the most senior employee in the Education Department for this region, in fact the Head, greeting first us, then Thongkhanh, with warm familiarity.

All of this is starting to fall into place in my mind as Ms. Houngkham Phengsavath sits down behind her desk and begins to leaf through a folder of notes and contracts, all of which are handwritten in the beautiful flowing script of the Lao language.

She glances up from the papers to slowly study the Phoujong villagers. We all straighten up slightly and there is respectful silence as she takes up a red pen. Occasionally she consults with either Buanthone or

Buanphong who pay careful attention to her remarks. Each page is read and corrected. Ms. Houngkham consults Thongkhanh. No one else speaks. Buanthone then leaves the room apparently to rewrite by hand what we have come to realize was the contract to build A School for Phoujong.

Ms. Houngkham eases back her chair to speak for a considerable length of time to Phoujong Headman Laisiew. She does this without pause enough for us to ask Chanthy what is being said. The calm considered tone of voice and continual eye contact are sufficient to make us understand that what she is saying is to be taken seriously. Once or twice Laisiew consults with his villagers from whom there is no dissent.

When Ms. Houngkham stands up, we all stand up. Buanthone, it is explained, will take some time to make the changes to the contract and for it to be typed up and we should return early in afternoon at which time the papers will be ready to sign. There is a pregnant pause during which I ask Ms. Houngkham if she would care to join us for lunch. She accepts graciously saying she will join us at the restaurant I had suggested, the best one in town but still simple for all that, in an hour's time. She would like to bring Buanthone and Bounpheng with her.

We all decamp on various motorbikes and other vehicles. The Phoujongers go ahead to the restaurant to let them know there will be a big party for lunch. The

NaLiners stop off at the simple guesthouse where we have taken a room and from which we need to pick up extra batteries and kip. Seated on hard timber benches with uncomfortable carved backs we space ourselves around a low table and piece together the gist of the morning's conversation between Ms. Houngkham and Headman Laisiew.

It seems she had let him know, in no uncertain terms, that the Phoujong villagers will be expected to pull their weight in this Project. They are to give of their labour and their time. They are to be helpful and supportive not only of Iain and I but of all the tradesmen and general hands who will be building their School. I hope she hadn't actually told them how fortunate they were to be even getting a school, but I don't ask because I was too cowardly to want to hear the answer.

When we try suggesting that of course the Phoujongers will be welcome on the same paid terms as other workers Mr. Khong speaks for the first time all morning. He quite obviously has strong feelings about what Ms. Houngkham has said. Through Chanthy, who is slightly embarrassed or at least uncomfortable with having to be the meat in this verbal sandwich Mr. Khong explains that for all schools built in Lao Loum villages the inhabitants are expected to donate their labour. Those who don't give freely with their hands for whatever reason: age, infirmity, necessary farm work,

43

family commitments or simply a matter of choice, were excused but in place of their labour they paid $2 a day into a fund. This discharge fee, a sizeable amount in Laos, went towards the building work.

The three of them, plus we two, know that no-one from Phoujong, a village far poorer than NaLin could possibly afford to pay a $2-a-day fee to have a school built. But we take Mr. Khong's information on board, along with his emphatic conclusion that he is not anticipating any assistance from the villagers. The tone of his voice suggests that in fact he would find them more trouble than they are worth. He continues by saying that as he was all but certain there was not one experienced tradesman in Phoujong they would be useful for manual labour only, though perhaps they could provide some of the formwork timber.

Ever the diplomat, Iain moves the conversation on and I notice Thongkhanh recognizes in Iain a brother in arms. It seems, Iain says in a conciliatory tone, that all going well there will be a contract to sign this afternoon. Perhaps before we did that it would be good to know what Mr. Khong's fee would be and what that amount would cover.

Though caught a little off-guard, Mr. Khong quickly gathers his wits and with the casual air of a man who hadn't given this a lot of thought, he purses his lips and moves his head back and forth as if mentally calculating this figure for the very first time.

Finally he announces a fee of 80 million kip (about US$10,000) and that this would include all labour, fully paid for by him. We, that is Iain and I, will be

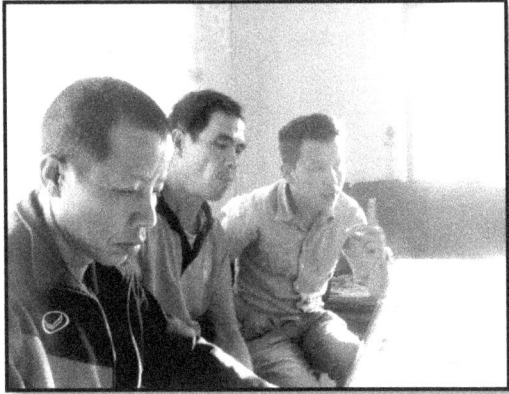

Thongkhanh, Mr. Khong and Chanthy as we discuss fees for the job.

required to provide all materials and also have them delivered as soon as required to the building site.

How long, Iain asks courteously, did Mr. Khong think the job would take? Again there are gestures to suggest that he hadn't given much thought to this either and I for one am rather impressed with his acting skills.

He pronounces, 'the end of the first week in April.' Everyone, including us, beams with pleasure. The all-important Pi Mai, Lao New Year Festival, is scheduled for mid-April. This timing means those involved can anticipate a Happy New Year. Though everyone knows that the entire Project and schedule are totally weather-dependent.

The luncheon is an unqualified success even though the people from the two villages remain distinct from

Lunch with the Education Department officials after signing the contracts

each other, again apart from Thongkhanh who mixes with easy grace amongst everyone. I sit next to Ms. Houngkham with Iain and Chanthy on the other side of the long table for ease of translation. She tells us what a positive difference the School at Phoujong will make. We thank her for making us welcome and tell her we will do the best job we can, not just for Phoujong and the Education Department but also for the generous donors at home. It is important that everyone understands we are not doing this with our own funds.

The Lao do not sit about at a meal table making idle small talk or solving the world's problems. The aim is to enjoy a sufficiency and once food is eaten, by using the fingers to make balls of sticky rice with which to then scoop up whatever is on offer, they are up and off to attend to whatever is in need. The men imbibe a couple of Beer Lao each and when Iain goes to pay the woman restaurant owner comments on how good it is that a school was being built at Phoujong. It seems as though everyone in Muang Nan now knows why we are in town. The bill for feeding the entire crowd comes to less than the equivalent of $50.

Later that afternoon we returned to Ms. Houngkham's office, and everyone signs a contract, though with whom and for what we of course haven't a clue because the whole schmozzle is written in Lao! There is, Ms. Houngkham tells us, just one adjustment the Department would like to make to the plans Iain had unfurled before her like a magician. The Teacher's Office, could it please be extended by 40cms. Not a problem. Everyone shakes hands in an egalitarian manner. No old-fashioned pre-Change of Government *nops* here. We never again saw anyone from the Department of Education until eight weeks later when the job was all but complete and we made plans for the official opening. Nor did we see any other person in an official capacity.

So much for our fears of being required to pay kickbacks.

Though I should mention that on the way into the restaurant Thongkhanh, who seems to know everyone, introduces us to the new District Governor, Sivone

Vongkhamchan, who has just replaced the one we had met over the deadly buffalo ears. This replacement has about him the air of one who was moving up the economic ladder. The haircut, the spiffy pale blue, well-cut linen jacket and trousers, the unctuous smile.

A month or so later a message from this man was relayed to us to say that he needed a new computer. Cheeky sod, we thought and did nothing.

However, when a friend of Chanthy's uncle who works in the Education Department makes a request through Chanthy for a ream of A4 paper, explaining that the Department in Muang Nan had run out of paper the previous month, we of course bring a couple down for him from LPB. Their total cost was all of $5.

A couple of days later another contract is signed, though this is a more personal one: a wedding contract. Builder Khong's middle child, 22-year-old daughter Zon, is to be married and we are invited to the celebrations.

The Bounsavath family has a home in Ban Namphai a village just off Route 12. Travelling south from LPB the turn down into this village is a kilometre or so before Muang Nan. This is our first visit and we decide immediately and simultaneously that if we were looking for a spot locally in which to build a house Namphai would be it. In real-estate-speak it is distant enough to retain a peaceful rural atmosphere while at the same time being conveniently close to the High School, daily morning market and general stores in the District Centre of Muang Nan. Added to which it is connected to the Centre by the recently much upgraded main road that links LPB with Sayaboury via the impressive bridge across the Mekong, partly financed by Korea.

Nestled in the rice paddy the village is shaded by a proliferation of luxuriant palm trees. But it is the attractively winding, though un-surfaced, laneways that create the appealing atmosphere. Lined on both sides by two-storey wooden houses with jutting balconies it takes very little imagination to conjure up an Italian hill town or a village in the West of England though from some two hundred years ago. Right now of course Namphai doesn't have the amenities these places provide. But it will, in perhaps a few decades, if our world manages to hang on by the spider's web fine thread presently connecting it to its shaky future.

In fact Namphai's future is indeed far more shaky than we could have ever have imagined on that visit. Four months later a dam wall, high above the village on the jungled hillside breaks, sending water, tonnes of it, gushing down, into and through the village. Two people are drowned and the destructive havoc destroys many houses. The ground floor of Mr. Khong's family home and everything in it is turned to useless mush. But all this will happen with callous indifference in an unforeseen future that perhaps fortunately none of us can ever see.

In the unsuspecting calm of the now it has been agreed with Mr. Khong, father of the bride, that payment for his work on The School at Phoujong will come in three tranches. The first third is to be paid immediately, the second about mid-way through the project and the third when the job is complete.

Salaries for Thongkhanh and Chanthy will be paid separately every two weeks. We are determined to set a standard of best practice. None of this making people wait for their due monies as happens in too many Lao Government Departments and private businesses. Establishing personal trust and mutual professional respect is a premium. So it is that we arrive at the wedding with Iain's daypack stuffed with bricks of crisp notes of Lao kip.

The dry legal formalities of the marriage would have taken place some days or even weeks previously in a government office in LPB. What we were witness to is the celebrations and what made this event different from most was that this is Zon's second wedding in under a year.

While marriages in Laos are not exactly arranged to the same degree as in, for instance, India it is for sure that the entire extended families of both bride and groom are involved in the decision making process. Though it is the bridegroom who is expected to bring financial and social clout to the relationship it is the bride's family who pay for the party on the day.

But even with everyone having their two bob's worth of input into the choice, mistakes can be made and Zon's first husband, now ex, quickly showed his true colours, we were told, as a lazy ne'er-do-well. Laziness and second chances are not options in a society where life is all too often foreshortened. Without more ado the marriage was cancelled. The bridegroom's payments returned before any irredeemable damage, such as a pregnancy, could occur. A new partner was chosen and we hoped for his, as well as everyone else's sake that he would measure up.

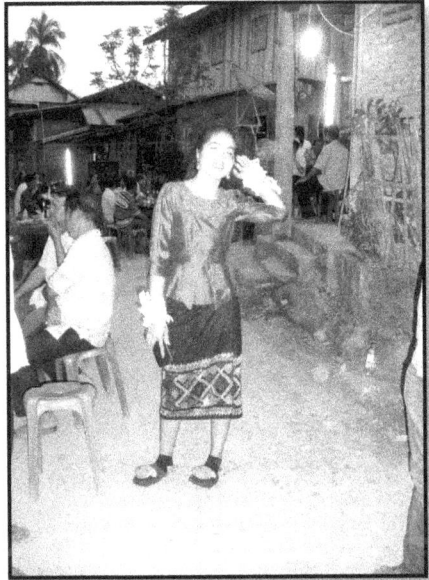

Zon at her wedding party

In the Khousanvath's main room that is crammed with mostly elderly female relatives and friends we make our *nops*, joined palms raised to the forehead and tuck our gift of banknotes into the blessing strings tied around Zon's

The wedding party in Namphai village

wrists noting that she looks as radiant as any bride wants to look on her wedding day. We then join a group of men sitting around one of the many tables outside that fill the main street.

Leaving Iain to a peer group pressure drinking competition with the fellows, I make my way to the area where the women are tucked away, squatting down on their supple haunches, creating lashings of food in large cauldrons.

They wave and beckon me to join them. Quite a few have obviously also been stuck into the turps and there is no way I could get away without slurping from the shared bottles. Everyone is in high humour.

There are dogs and chooks and ducks underfoot and scores of children dressed in their best and wanting to ogle the *falang* with pale cropped hair.

The noise is like a stifling wrap-around blanket...

and that's before the 'music' starts up, distorted and at full-throttle.

We join the table at which Thongkhanh is sitting, beer in hand, while he quite apparently explains to many others our connection with the Khousanvath family. Petite Grandma Buachanh, wearing her best blue silk top, is walking about at a slight distance cradling a miraculously sleeping Jarrah in her arms, while his mother Bounlee, it is explained, is helping with the cooking.

Food dishes come in quick succession and are consumed promptly. The dogs and livestock waste not a scrap. The dead Beer Lao bottles mount up.

We know that the next treat is the dancing and are very relieved when Mr. Khong emerges from the melee, looking as smart as every father-of-the-bride should look and Iain tells him we have the first tranche of his monies and would like to hand it over. He too seems pleased to be able to take a breather from the exhausting business of becoming a father-in-law again and after checking with his wife as to where the kip could be safely stored, it is agreed that a cousin... every Lao has a myriad of such relatives... could keep it in his safe at his shop back up on the main road.

Leaving the party to do this takes a lingering while but eventually we are all sitting on upturned cartons of comestibles imported from Thailand outside this cousin's small general store and Mr. Khong is expertly flicking, as do all Lao, backwards through the wads of banknotes.

A huge starlit sky arced above us and as the wife of the cousin, in whose house the safe is located...it is always, as I was to learn, the women who handle the monies... deposited it all in her safe, convoys of trucks roar by, unnervingly close, in the darkness on their way to and from the border with China.

Mr. Khong writes a receipt in Lao, we all shake hands and with no further ado the deal is settled and he returns to the party. Work will begin tomorrow.

4 FOUNDATIONS

The cursed blessing of the Internet came up trumps. On Howtopedia Iain discovered a site: *How To Build A School In Developing Countries*. No kidding! Download for free. Perhaps, as you can work out how to build a nuclear bomb via the Internet, this could be described as the upside.

It's an excellent site crammed with really useful information and suggestions from building design and materials through the entire construction process. All of it imminently sensible and obviously written by people who have come to know their stuff because they have first hand experience. It covers the necessities for building in the full gamut of geographical and social situations and it pulls no punches. There are no glib politically correct aphorisms. It is all very simple, clearly laid out and down to earth. Our now grubby, dog-eared printed copy became like a beginner's bible with orange highlights and we carried it with us throughout the experience. Thank you.

Iain also dinged up *Toilets*, finding a myriad of sites offering a confusing choice. For weeks before we left for Laos almost all conversation centred on defecation and urination. Our friends were very tolerant and several of them even became enthused.

Iain was for a while sidetracked, or perhaps the more appropriate phrase is bogged down, by the latest pooh technology. This is *SLIPS*, the acronym standing for *Slippery Liquid-infused Porous Surfaces*. Of course it is American, occasionally you have to love them, and from no less august an institution than Harvard University. The advertising copy reads 'Harvard's *SLIPS* technology solves sticky situations.'

The idea is based on biomimicry; think how the wily pitcher plant attracts insects to its invitingly generous mouth which is slimed with a very thin layer of water that allows no traction and makes it impossible for an insect once landed to back out.

The idea involves coating a naturally sticky surface, wood, metal or plastic with a solid layer that attracts a liquid layer that makes it permanently wet and creates an ultra-slippery surface that repels blood, bacteria, dust, water, ice, cement and more;

the more in our situation being faeces and urine. As the saying goes, there's money in muck, and SLIPS has already attracted $3 million in initial funding.

Another university research project, was Australian and therefore came with a more down to earth name, *Not Just a Hole in the Ground*. This pit toilet concept came up for a lot of detailed discussion over our breakfast table. I have to admit I was initially attracted to the concept because of the fun graphics on the site.

Then there was the Clivas Multrum toilet. This had great appeal, as it was self-composting. We even drove out into the bush to meet with the Self-Composting King himself, Garry Scott. He has installed over a thousand of these appliances in an area from Grafton to the Queensland border, a distance of 400 kms. and talked reverentially about them. It was case of Love me, Love my Loo. Garry took us to the side of his family home and showed us in close-up detail how every second day or so he takes the lid off the storage box to run his fingers through what had been deposited, months previously, so as to break it up for easier composting.

Perhaps we could be written off as unadventurous, but after some months of literal hands-on research, plus a continual stream of discursive conversation we finally plumped for a regular septic system.

SLIPS was still in development, though we were mad enough to imagine approaching them as 'early-adopters' with the suggestion that we could become part of their research project. Not Just a Hole in the Ground almost made it but we didn't have a clue about what sort of soil Phoujong was built on or where the run-off would go And the Clivas Multrum? Who would maintain it? Who was going to explain what this involved? Personal ablutions are a very private affair in situations where people have no sanitation facilities.

Until now the schoolchildren of Phoujong along with all the villagers simply used the surrounding forest. This is done so discreetly that I was never aware of anyone using the adjacent bush as a latrine.

Our loo, as it had become designated, would be the first such facility in Phoujong, so we decided it was a case of Keep it Simple Stupid and build a regular septic. Iain went to work creating detailed drawings again brightened with orange highlighter.

***

Building work begins without fanfare. With the site cleared and leveled, there is no official turning of the first sod with a new shovel, no ribbon to cut, no speeches made. Mr. Khong, looking none the worse for wear following his daughter's marriage celebrations, simply drives up the rutted track in his open-backed truck in the back of which is a pre-loved cement mixer. This is to be the only cement mixer used during the entire of building of the School. By the end of the process it had become cemented to the spot and looked decidedly as though it needed a long holiday

A group of workmen from his village are already waiting for him and watched by numerous curious schoolboys... still no girls as yet...they offload this machine. Then by following behind Mr. Khong's unraveling ball of string, pegging it at designated spots, the

The lone cement mixer arrives

outline of the building is established. At the end of this first day narrow foundation trenches have been dug by following under this string line and deep holes dug where they intersect. Suddenly the shape and size building-to-be becomes comprehensible.

Also by the end of that day Thongkhanh has already ordered large amounts of sand and gravel and the first of many, many bags of cement. Taking the advice of serial school

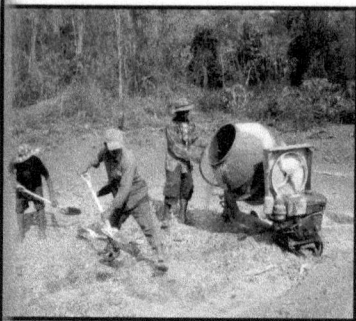

Cement deliveries and the mixer swings into gear

builders and ever-helpful friends Dao and Stephen Midgely we go for the Elephant brand Thai produced cement, even though this is somewhat more expensive than the Lao version. Dao and Stephen, a forty-year marriage of Lao/Australian heritages make very clear to us that cheaper is not always better. The previous year we had attended the opening of their three-large-room school with triple septic system toilets on the outskirts of LPB. All this and more built with funds raised privately in Australia. At the beginning of this visit we have been at the opening of their two-schoolroom extension with its impressive four-cubicle toilet. It is a relief and delight to talk with people who relate to loos with a depth and passion that can only be fully felt by those who have built so many! This year's beauty by the Midgleys was built to service a 1000 pupil high school at Kok Ngiew a few hours north of LBP and near to Nong Kiau. This small settlement clings to the banks of the River Ou. It is popular with the close-knit international fraternity of keen foreign rock climbers because it centres on a dramatic bulge of a rock-face that rears temptingly out of the swift flowing waters. Tempting that is to those who enjoy such challenges. Visitors to the local township also included a group of non-climbers at the riverside guesthouse where we all stayed. That evening, in the dining room, they unavoidably learnt a great deal more than they bargained for, as Dao regaled us with a blast of salty stories about her experiences while building their latest school.

Thongkhanh carefully annotates all of these deliveries of materials in the hard-covered ruled notebook Iain had presented him with, along with a selection of pens and markers and his first ever wages. Thongkhanh took to his role as Building Site Supervisor with verve

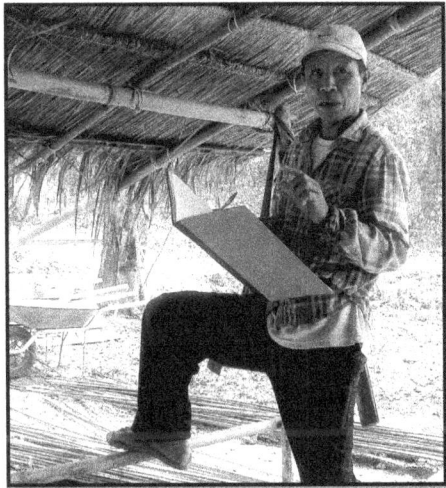

Thongkhanh with his ledger book

and determination. Nothing was ever too far, too big

or little, too difficult or demanding for him. Throughout the building process he never let anyone down, most importantly himself. Whatever needed doing, whoever needed that extra bit of help, Thongkhanh was always there, oftentimes it seemed before a difficulty had even been articulated. He had a knack of anticipating problems and making them disappear before they could get out of control.

Bang with her spinning wheel

Thongkhanh was born in 1967, during a period when governance in Laos was extremely unstable. His mother, Bang, already had eleven children, among them, Thongkhanh, when her husband was killed in a shooting accident while hunting for food.. She married again but when this husband became an alcoholic they were divorced. With a third husband, Chanh, whom we had met many times over these years, she had one more child. When this husband died last year, nine of her children were still living and Bang, by then 74, had come to represent for me the embodiment of grace

62

under pressure and survival despite all.

Thongkhanh married very young, as almost all Lao did, particularly then, when they had all seen so much death and devastation. It was a seemingly basic human instinct to reproduce and cram as much as possible into life before it was snatched away.

For generations the extended Sisombuth family had lived hand to mouth as rice farmers. But somehow through the turmoil of these battle-fatigued years Thongkhanh, with the strength of character that we were to witness these decades later, glimpsed other possibilities. He dreamed of belonging to the spearhead of the developing new nation and in addition to working in the family rice paddy he underwent the simple training available then in order to become a teacher. The problem was that though there were Government teaching positions available, there was no pay. Thongkhanh struggled on, determined not to give up his dream. He continued unpaid teaching as well as doing his share in the family fields. By

The hut in NaLin village where Chanthy was born

63

now his wife Buachanh already had two children, Jai and Chanthy with a third, Bounlee on the way.

Then the gods struck in the haphazard manner for which they are renowned. Thonghkhanh became very sick, to the point of being incapacitated. For some months he teetered on the brink. There are a myriad death-inducing illness to which the very poor are especially prey in the tropics. Perhaps it was malaria, or yellow fever or dengue. All Chanthy remembers is that his Father's death seemed imminent and that when he finally, after some long months, came back from edge Buachanh insisted that sadly her husband was a generation too early and that they both should focus their energies on growing enough rice to raise their family of three and ensuring they, at least, received enough education to fulfill their Father's dream in life's continuous grinding mill.

NaLin's ageing wooden wat

In the face of this needful acceptance for Buachanh there was the solace of her Buddhist faith. When we first became a part of the family we saw that she washed and put on a clean sarong at the end of a day's manual work and then before beginning to prepare the family's evening meal she always, without fail, took an offering to NaLin's decomposing wooden wat, where she made her prayers and gave a meal to the one resident monk.

Thongkhanh did not accompany her. Perhaps his Buddhist beliefs had grown beyond the need for these daily rituals though he certainly had remained a deeply Buddhist man. In truth, he is the most Buddhist person we have ever known, that is if being Buddhist really does entail having a serenely open, generous heart and mind.

Now it was through his three offspring that this good man's dreams and goals were being achieved. The expression on his face when Chanthy translated conversations at meetings with officials or at bargaining sessions with builders' suppliers manifested his joy in how far this formerly scrawny runt of a lad had hoiked himself beyond the rice paddies.

Neither will we forget Thongkhanh's words when Iain handed him his initial wage. He gave his boyishly broad grin as he hefted it in his hands and through his son told us, 'I have never been paid this much money in my entire life. Please give it to my wife.'

That evening we travel back down from the edge of the forest and on past the little turn-off into NaLin, along 'The Road' that had been built with monies from our initial fund-raising in Australia two years previously. To reach Muang Nan was always a bone-jarring at least one- hour journey and one on which I was always shamelessly glad about my age and my sex because these seemingly entitled me to first dibs at a seat in the driver's cabin. As the weeks went by these bodily facts were added to by my obviously increasing physical incapacity. I attempted, I truly did, to not play the little old disabled lady card, but my word, was I relieved when the various drivers insisted on me getting in beside them. It was still an uncomfortable ride but nothing like as tough as for anyone being bounced about on the floor of the truck's tray back.

On this first evening's journey we have a soft-ish ride, though at first it seemed that we might not get a ride at all and we had visions of sleeping rough on the cracked mud floor of the old schoolhouse. Thongkhanh had called on his constantly used mobile phone to everyone he could think of in NaLin village to try to cadge us a ride. He had even resorted to attempting to summon up people he knew in more distant Muang Nan. No one it seemed was available, not even for the negotiated fee that was always around $18. Suddenly it seemed everyone had something happening that precluded them from

66

transporting the two *falang*, plus his son, back to their hostelry in the District Centre, Muang Nan.

We were conscious of there being something else at play and at Thongkhanh's embarrassment over this and were attempting to make light of the situation by saying we were fine to sleep on the bare floor when Sanfin drove up. You may remember him as the Scowler at the meeting with the people from the Education Department. Did that really only happen a few days previously or had it happened on another planet in another life? So much had been jam-packed into these already cruelly hot days.

Knowing that he had us over a barrel, Sanfin made his demand for $25 accompanied by his best dark scowl, pointing out that his truck...and I know you will want to know its make, etc, but such niceties totally escape my attention, was new and also clean. What we didn't know, when we accepted his 'kind offer' was that although the truck was indeed new, so was the driver and that this was in fact the first time Sanfin had ever driven. Some things are clearly better left unknown.

But Sanfin was not ready to leave immediately. Before that happened he insisted, insisting was another of his habits along with the scowl, on negotiating with Thongkhanh about the price of timber for the formwork for the foundations of the

School and pylons necessary for the next building phase. It had been agreed, though we had been unaware of this, that the villagers of Phoujong would provide this timber, from trees felled in the forests around their village. We were also later to learn that a permit needed to be obtained from an unspecified Government department for this felling to occur legally. But the always-tetchy non-relationship between the villagers and any Government official more or less precluded this from occurring. Timber getting and sawing always happened deep in the forest away from the prying eyes of officials who may well have demanded payment, personal or otherwise, for this permission. Or even just refused permission.

We attempted to stand inconspicuously to one side as the bargain was struck. Thongkhanh had this enviable ability to appear pleasingly self-effacing while in fact sticking to his guns despite Sanfin's bullyboy tactics. The price, 1.8 million kip, or US $225, was finally set and we agreed to pay the monies as soon as Mr. Khong told us the timber was of acceptable quality. This meant it was the right length and width and also straight, with no deforming bows or twists.

At last we were off, with all four of us in the cabin, Chanthy tucked into the cramped space behind the driver's seat and our bench seat. The translated conversation got off to a tense start when Sanfin asked us if we had spoken since our arrival with Mr. P. I am going to use only the first letter of his name because I don't wish to cause him embarrassment. Not that he will read this but perhaps people who would recognize him will.

In a small digression I should explain that when we were first contacted by Mr. P., who lived with his Lao wife in a suburb in south Brisbane, we were delighted to think that we had breached the wall that seemed to enclose the Lao immigrant community living in Australia. He had heard of the improvements we had managed to achieve for NaLin and that we were now hoping to build a School for Phoujong. We met him and his wife and gave him a number of the three calendars I had created using my own photographs. I hoped to sell them in Australia and in Laos to raise further funds. The conversation then turned to his health that, he informed us, was not good. For this reason he was returning to Laos for the first time since immigrating to Australia as a refugee in 1975 at the Change of Government. Unhappy with the treatment suggested by Australian doctors he planned to seek help in his Homeland.

We had heard no more from Mr. P for six months or so when he telephoned to tell us he was back in Australia, would like to give us around $150 for the calendars he had sold and would also like more of them to sell. On this second visit he showed us, well actually Iain really, because he never included me in conversations, photographs of a hands-on healing he had undergone in Laos. He then presented a small rusty tin container from which he tipped out a number of small metal clips and other assorted bits and pieces. These he informed us, had been removed from his stomach, the centre of the pain he had been experiencing, by a Special Man. This removal had not involved opening the body or organs nor had it left a scar on the flesh.

That was okay by us. After all it takes all sorts and the main thing was that Mr. P was no longer in pain. He sold more calendars for which his wife gave us the money because by this time Mr. P had gone up to Laos on another visit for further hands-on treatment. This time he contacted Chanthy to say he was in Sayaboury and would like to meet up when he came to LPB. There had been a few sporadic telephone calls but he would never leave a number or name of a place where Chanthy could contact him. I just hoped he hadn't died from treatment or non-treatment either of which was an equal possibility.

Well obviously he hadn't and not only was he alive but he was in Ban Nan Nuan, the furthest settlement beyond Phoujong, a distance of at least a further twenty kilometres over the roughest track I have ever seen anywhere and from where, if indeed he really was there, Mr. P was intent on making trouble.

During that ride it became apparent that Mr. P. had given Sanfin and through him the entire population of Phoujong, the impression that we were very wealthy Australians who could be tapped for limitless funds.

Why he would have said this we were completely unable to work out. Perhaps it was a way of big noting himself by insinuating that he had done so well in his new country that he mixed in the company of the extremely wealthy. After all in the eyes of many of his compatriots he had fled his country in its darkest hour. So bringing us back with him, which was how he had explained our presence in Phoujong to the villagers, was his shot at redemption.

At first we try to laugh off this suggestion of limitless monies as ludicrous but this only darkens Sanfin's scowl. Then we attempt to explain what had gone into raising the funds, from scores of hard-working, mostly Australian, people to build the School. But Sanfin will not have a bar of that either. His misconception would not have mattered one jot except for the fact that Sanfin and his extended family were important people in Phoujong. As we were to discover, when they spoke others listened and fell into line.

Poverty is not the great equalizer any more than is wealth. When the layer of slippery ice between survival and going under becomes so precariously thin as to be all but transparent, the hard scrabble for survival reveals characteristics that are more easily concealed by those further up the economic chain. The people who live in Phoujong are poor, perhaps even the poorest of the poor. In Sanfin it was possible for them to see at least a small degree of the financial success most of them craved.

Sanfin had earned this following in Phoujong's small society by hard work. Married and with two small children he had taken a job across the border in a Thai factory. This is a decision made by numerous Lao people, sometimes by choice but often under pressure from family members. Commonly people smugglers are involved, especially in the case of young girls who are taken to work in the brothels of Chiangmai, Pattaya and Bangkok.

For men long hours of repetitive manual labour under poor conditions are the norm. Sanfin would have shared a dormitory room with a score or more of other employees, most probably Lao of the same ethnicity. Hot-bunking, which describes the use of a narrow cot across the full twenty-four hours with one sleeper getting in after a work-shift replacing another worker going on-shift. No safety regulations. No holiday pay. Seven days a week.

He had returned recently with enough cash money

to enable him to build a brick home. In Laos, as in many parts of the world, brick is cheaper now than timber. Sanfin's house also had a tin rather than thatch roof and was on the farthest edge of the village. In addition he had bought the vehicle in which he is now driving us back down to Muang Nan.

We pay the requested fee and invite him to join us for dinner at one of the several little cafes on the main street before making his return journey. He accepted but the scowl never left his face. During the meal his mobile rings twice. On both occasions it was Mr. P. We could only assume he was filling his protégé with even more intoxicating poison about our river of monies.

That night both Iain and I lay and mulled over the possible deleterious effects Mr. P. might have on our relationships with the people of Phoujong. We could not help but feel distress. The following morning as we slurped our habitual breakfast bowl of steaming *pho pak* at the bus station cafe, he continued to be the topic of conversation then Chanthy let drop, with a degree of embarrassment, that perhaps Mr.P. was trying to impress his girlfriend.

'Girlfriend! What girlfriend?' Iain is astounded.

'A young girl in Nan Nuan.' Chanthy's awkwardness deepened.

73

'How young?' Iain wants to know, 'and how long has this been happening?'

'Perhaps sixteen. He met her in Sayaboury where she was visiting friends. That was a year ago. He has followed her here to her home village of Nan Nuan and brings her presents. He says he wants to marry her.'

So. Now we had it. A man past his prime, thinking with his dick and seeking to win a young girl by telling her he has wealthy associates in Australia and could make things happen for her. An old, old story. How very corny. I am embarrassed for Mr. P. but only for a few seconds. We wished that Chanthy had told us all this before, though we respect his decision not to. Gossip, loose talk and Buddhism are not a match.

Less than a week later Chanthy tells us that Sanfin has been involved in an accident. 'He was driving back up the track to Phoujong and he lost control of the wheel and his truck ended up on its side in a ditch.' We weren't so heartless as to not feel sorry for Sanfin. It seemed that he had broken his arm in a couple of places and there had been considerable damage to his new vehicle.

'It's the *phi*,' Iain smiles a little awkwardly. I have been thinking exactly that but hadn't wanted to voice these thoughts to my usually totally skeptical partner. Chanthy agrees immediately and then with deep belief, adds, 'If you do bad things then bad things happen to you,'

The *phi*, a constant source of possible menace in the lives of all Lao whether they are Buddhist or animist are negative forces that lie in wait for an opportunity to wreak havoc. The fact that Sanfin was an inexperienced driver negotiating a difficult track could of course have given assistance to the *phi*. But there again that's what *phi* do; they hop in to take advantage of a situation.

I have reported this story about Mr. P. and Sanfin because I don't want you to get the wrong idea by thinking this whole project was all sweetness and light or anything as soppy as that. But that's enough.

On the local bus we took back up to LPB the following day we all three of us agreed that we'd put all thoughts about Mr. P. and his possible negative effects out of our minds and concentrate only on the positive aspects and there were a lot of those.

5 BREAKTHROUGH

It was the dresses that did it. Thank you Ms. Babette. Ten days into the project it was still only the boys who were confident enough to come on site during the midday break or after class was over, to clamber in and around the footings and get a close-up look at what was happening.

Then we bring out Ms. Babette's donated dresses to be given by Teacher Kaojien to eleven of his female students. It is a delight to watch the excitement of the girls who are chosen as recipients and equally heart-warming to watch the reaction of the rest of the girls and boys. Of course, as they are human, there must have been some degree of upset that they missed out. But there are no signs of the petulance or envy I had anticipated and which would surely have been apparent in more affluent places where a gifted dress would more likely have been a quickly discarded one-minute-wonder. But here, where a crisp, cotton dress smelling of newness is a unique experience, the chosen girls are oohed and aahed over by the other pupils as a shared joy-filled experience. Then they do that thing all females do world-wide, when they have on something new and that they know they look pretty in; they twirl and sashay and smile, before running outside to show themselves off. It's a girl thing, a sense of self-worth perhaps. I have seen it happen in other battered places.

From then on the building site becomes their playground too, joining in along with the boys. Of course we let the girls who didn't receive dresses know that we would try to bring them ones on our next visit and that we would also think of something for the boys.

Babette's dresses: girls will be girls

The men work on, either ignoring or finding a way around these fast-moving small people. We only witnessed perhaps three occasions during the building process in which students were shooshed away and those occurred when the children were endangering themselves with either the cement mixer, the big ten-gallon drum filled with water or the

Children watching

small generator that was used to fire up building tools in this electricity-less village. The dogs and even the pigs and chickens were also let roam.

We are delighted with this freedom for the children because we like to imagine that this experience of being close up and personal with the intricacies of creating a building from scratch could possibly make such an impression that two or even if its only one, of the thirty-three students will be inspired to think, 'I would like to do that.'

Another delight was re-meeting Bounyang. On our visit here last year we had noticed this then seven-year-old boy at the edge of the group that was being read to by Sinxai a member of a four-person crew from the National Library that was bringing books to the School.

Bounyang was a thin stick of a lad with a hacking cough whose dark eyes started from his head showing bewilderment and pain but also determination and intelligence. He had no use of his legs and could only move about by dragging himself across the sun-baked mud. How he managed in the long wet season didn't bear thinking about, still less his further future. Something had to be done to improve his desperate situation. His beautiful mother Mi had three other children ranging in age from three months to ten years. Without recourse to Project funds we arranged for his father Xienguanh to bring his son on the bus with us to LPB. At the hospital there, a place you wouldn't visit unless you were dying and it was your only choice, Bounyang was diagnosed as suffering from

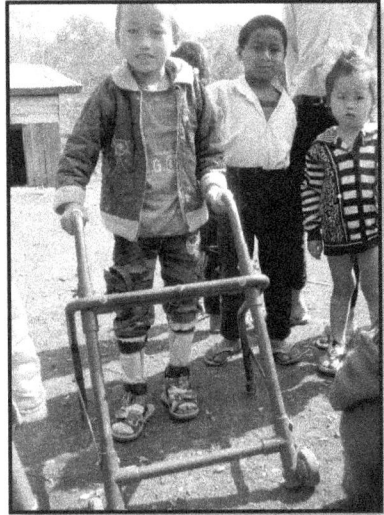

Bounyang with his walker

severe malnutrition and pneumonia. How well I can recall the drip-line being fed into the shriveled vein in his pitiably thin arm and how he didn't flinch, cry or even turn his head away because he simply didn't have the energy.

The hospital also diagnosed early childhood exposure to polio, a disease that has been eradicated in most parts of the world. They treated his struggling lungs, then fitted him up with calipers and with the use of a walking frame Bounyang returned home. Here he is almost a year later getting around on the building site and up and down across the steep gully that separates the School on the hill from the village proper. The other students automatically look out for him and give him a hand when he needs it but Bounyang still displays that determined spirit we had noticed when we first met him. Of course there are huge hurdles for him to overcome in a society that keeps itself fed by growing its own food. He will never be able to work in his family's fields. His only hope is to use the intelligence that has also remained very apparent.

His face lit up when he first saw us again. For an addicted hugger like me, Laos can sometimes be a tough call. But I somehow manage to get down on my knees beside him and not to weep with pleasure but to simply smile in return and put my hand on top of his as he grasps his frame.

****

During the few days we have been up in LPB eating restorative meals, having haircuts, sending round-up emails to supporters and redrawing architect Justin's plans to show more accurately what has now been jointly decided on as the final version, timber formwork has been brought on site by the Phoujongers. Mr. Khong had given it the skeptical eye and declared that about eighty percent of it measured up to his stringent quality demands mostly about

80

there being no warping. He is a tough nut and that is good of course for getting the best value for money for the Project but leaves Iain with the somewhat uncomfortable role of having to negotiate with Headman Laisiew.

All of them being men there is naturally quite a deal of ego involved, which is exhausting, especially in this heat. But it all gets sorted and Iain hands over payment from his backpack.

In an impressive tried and true building method not seen in Australia but always used in Laos the main slab is not laid first but last, after the superstructure is complete and the roof on. Some twenty-one metre-deep square holes are dug around and across the site to provide concrete and steel reinforced bases for the same number of steel and concrete pillars that will support the whole structure.

More of the metal rods are in the process of being cut to size, bent into shape and bound together with tie-wires to form small platforms that fit snugly into each of these square holes on top of a bed of concrete and gravel. Extra gravel and concrete will then be poured over the top of these platforms. The formwork, held in place by the concrete, will contain lengths of reinforcing rods knitted together to create strong steel-reinforced pylons.

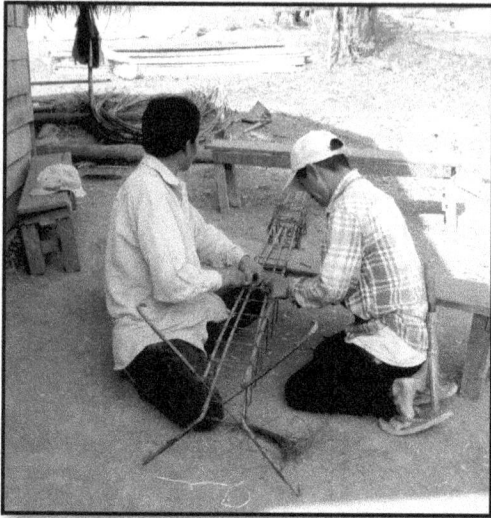

Tying together the steel reinforcing rods for the concrete pylons

An above ground interlacing network of these same steel rods are laid in wooden formworks placed between these deep holes. These too will be filled with a concrete and gravel mix to give the building its base strength.

For all this work, large bundles of reinforcing rods have been delivered from a supplier in Muang Nan and manhandled into place. Concrete blocks will create the outside as well as the internal walls on which the timber roofing framework will rest.

All this intense work has been made possible by a steady stream of bags of cement brought up from Muang Nan in groaning trucks. Offloading these bags is another physically demanding job.

Those men not lugging cement, at least ten of them, Khong included, are sitting in whatever shade they can find, toiling over the rather fiddly task of creating the metal skeletons for the pylons. There are no hierarchical labour demarcation lines. Everybody does everything, working as a team. Throughout the entire building process there is always a great atmosphere of camaraderie and humour.

Builder Khong promises us that if the threatening clouds don't dump their load of rain on us we can expect to see the first pylon pour later that afternoon.

Leaving Iain and Chanthy to go through the paperwork for other costs and accounts with Thongkhanh, I walk down into to the village, ludicrously trying to think myself into the role of a low-viz casual visitor out for a pleasant stroll. The village lies silently baking in the oppressive heat. Even the pigs and chickens have given up rootling about for scraps and are flopped out in the dust. Most residents are still working in their fields but there are a few women squatting on tiny handmade stools in the shade of an overhang. They don't make any overt signs of welcome but undaunted and perhaps driven by the heat and the need to sit down I indicate I would like to join them. One in the group produces an extra stool. My knees creak loudly as I hunker down beside her as best I can and it is at this point that something magical happens.

The woman is embroidering tiny stitches with coloured cotton thread onto a cloth dyed a deep blue with indigo. Only a small area peeps out from its dust and dirt protective wrapping. I express admiration for her work and this encourages her to unroll the complete piece. The beauty is such a blow to my senses I actually feel transported. It is as if the colours are singing. How can it be that in the midst of this degrading living situation she has managed to hold on to her cultural heritage to such an extent that she has created this story symphony of wonder. Because it is quite apparent that what she is sharing with me has more resonance than a rote handicraft done to simply fill in idle hours.

Perhaps it is the way in which she touches the piece with an otherworldly grace. She appears to glow, not with an emotion as simplistic and crass as pride, but with the knowledge she is making something beyond herself. She holds up a splendour of colours, predominantly blue but there is also white, red, green and yellow. It is almost a metre long. Her smile, as I express my astonishment, is inward, slow and deep.

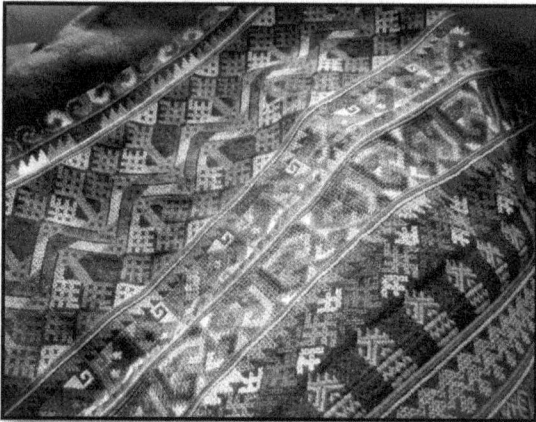

Embroidery up close

84

Just as quickly as it had appeared, the embroidered cloth is rewrapped and disappears like a conjurer's rabbit into a hat. The woman stands up and I get the feeling I have been permitted to see too much and am being dismissed. But as she walks away she turns her head and gestures for me to follow. We cross the squalor of the litter-strewn caked mud and approach another shack I recognize as being the home of teacher Kaojien. It is distinguishable from the other homes by having characters of Chinese calligraphy drawn in chalk down one side of the doorway.

As we arrive Kaojien's wife, Merynguen, steps out from the gloom and greets my guide who, it is immediately apparent from their strong facial similarities, is her sister. There is a brief conversation before Merynguen slips briefly back inside and returns with a parcel wrapped in a similar way to her sister's embroidered piece. With no further ado she rapidly unwraps and holds up in the harsh sunlight a pair of loose pants, both legs embroidered all around back and front and from waistband to hemline with compact rows of what I would in my ignorance

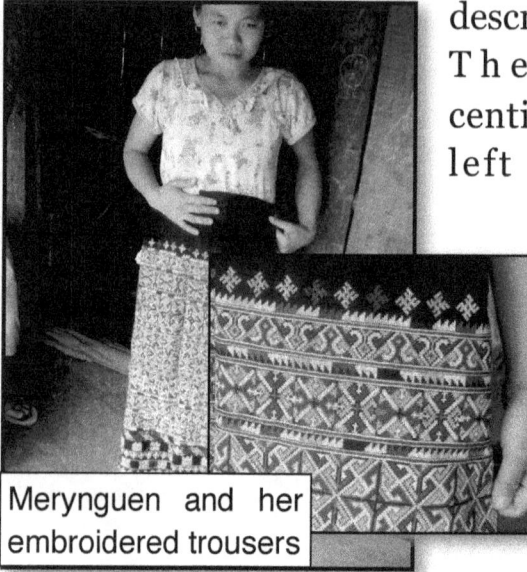

Merynguen and her embroidered trousers

describe as cross-stitch. There is not one centimeter of material left un-worked. The embroidery is so dense it gives the effect of the trousers being embossed. The same five colours, blue, white, red, green and yellow, but in this masterpiece the dominant colour is white. The sisters look at me in silence as I gape in awe.

Trying wildly to grasp what I am seeing and to honour their talent I say the name of what I believe is their ethnicity, Hmong. Both women shake their head.

'Yao,' Merynguen says fiercely.

'Yao', her sister confirms.

'Yao,' I repeat with some embarrassment.

'Yao Mien,' Merynguen elaborates and wanting to be sure I fully understand the significance of my cultural error she repeats, 'Yao Mien.'

***

In the highly idiosyncratic world of Creation Myths the Yao Story is up there with the best of them. The world was created by Pan Ku but a local ruler, King Ping, feeling under serious threat by a challenger to his throne lets it be widely known that whoever can rid him of this would-be usurper will be given extensive lands and the hand in marriage of his most beautiful youngest daughter. After some time as well as some substantial struggles, all of which the story relates in detail, a fellow arrives at court bearing the severed head of the King's enemy and demands the promised reward. The unexpected aspect of this so far commonplace fairytale is that the creature holding the head is a dog. A multi-coloured dog. Yes, you anticipated correctly; the same five colours as have ever since been used in Yao embroidery: blue, white, red, green and yellow. These are also of course Buddhism's traditional colours. But I don't think it would be the go for some clever-dick *falang* to inquire into why this might be so. In some stories the Dog looses his tail before the nuptials, in another version he doesn't. In some he even metamorphoses totally into human form. Common to all stories is that from this union of Divine Being/Dragon Dog, P'an Hung, and a Princess sprang forth six boys and six girls, the first dozen human ancestors of the Yao nation. It is also widely believed that P'an Hung will come to assist the Yao in their time of need.

I had returned to LPB somewhat embarrassed and chastened that I had accepted as fact that the villagers of Phoujong were all Hmong, the minority ethnicity most widely known outside Laos, though they in fact make up 8% of the total Lao population while the Khmu form 11%. The Yao number only 20,000 in a population of six and a half million for the whole country.

At one level did it really matter whether the villagers were Yao, or the Hmong and Khmu mix of groups we had accepted as given information? Phoujongers remained poor, discriminated against by the majority Lao people and in desperate need of, among much else, a decent school building.

In fact the Yao do have two major areas of commonality with the Hmong; they are Animist, not Buddhist as are the majority of Lao and they were 'an efficient friendly force' on the side of the American military during the bloodbath complexities of the America/VietNam/Laos debacles of the 1960s and 70s. The majority Lao people have not moved on from what they continue, naturally enough, to see as a form of treachery. They also remain derisive of people whose religious life encompasses the spirits of all living things, even though the Lao too embrace Animism alongside their more structured Buddhist beliefs. The Lao take the view that they   are the nation's central people and all others, members of the

130 numerically smaller ethnicities, exist merely on the edge of their Lao world. Sound familiar?

Given the quite evident underlying tensions between Phoujongers and outsiders, we felt we now understood a little more about them, to the point of at least accepting the fact that they do little to help their own cause. Perhaps experience has taught them not to have a cause. The villagers of Phoujong sure as hell remain prickly and somewhat distant. There was no openhearted embrace of us as there had been in NaLin. Experience over the centuries has turned them into damaged goods and we decided the best we could do was remain open to them and to start by attempting to learn more about how they got to be this way.

The Yao, who came originally from China's Yang Tse basin became a recognized distinct ethnic group in China during the T'ang Dynasty that was in power from 618 to 907. This fact establishes their culture as being older than even the Han, the present group who are today China's majority people.

As the Mongols and the Han, increasing in numbers and power, began throwing their weight around, the Yao moved south. Numerous other groups of various ethnicities, including the Hmong, did the same. Perhaps at the time, the size of China appeared so limitless that when your neighbours became pushy, moving away looked like the answer. They settled in Hunan, Guanxi, Yunnan, Guangdong, Guizhou and Jiangxi.

But the invaders kept on their tail and finally the Yao stood their ground and fought on the loosing side in the Taiping Rebellion, a bitter war that lasted for a decade and a half beginning in 1850. From then on the Yao were on the run, crossing the mountains into the northern parts of VietNam Thailand and Laos in what still remains a pseudo-homeland area of somewhat porous ill-defined borders.

It could be proposed that those who stayed in China, and their following generations, who now number around two and a half million, made a better choice. Shortly after the founding of the Peoples Republic of China in 1949 the national government defined the Yao as a discrete nationality. Over the following years more than 2000 Yao autonomous counties, towns and administrative villages were established under a policy of equality for all nationalities. Again in 1979 Yao rights and privileges as a distinct nationality were confirmed. We have spent some time in these parts of China and seen how strong the cultures of many ethnicities are there, though it has to be said that the Han dominates the entire country and people belonging to the 55 other recognized groupings lag far behind in economic terms.

Once settled in their tiny villages secreted in the borderlands amongst the camouflage of the limestone peaks, the Yao set themselves up to do what they have done for centuries, catch wild birds and animals such as cats, snakes, rats and frogs and grow dry rice for themselves, corn as feed for their livestock as well as growing opium as a cash crop.

All of this they have in common once more with the Hmong. The difference occurs with religious practices. The Hmong are Animists, almost pure and simple, whereas Yao animist beliefs are deeply overlaid with the Taoism picked up from their centuries of living cheek by jowl with the Chinese. In common with the Chinese they have a tonal language and their religious texts are written in Chinese. This makes their beliefs and practices stronger than any other minority people in Asia. They keep memorial tablets showing complex family trees of their ancestors for whom they care, in a spiritual sense, through to the sixth generation. They have religious paintings, elaborate costumes, silver jewelry and hand-painted manuscripts. They also have a literary tradition of song and legend, bury their dead and believe in reincarnation.

In these complicated ethnic structures and overlay of mixed cultures there are two branches of the Yao. The more populous Yao Mien, to which Phoujong's embroidering sisters were insistent I understood they belong, and the Yao Mun. The separation between these two occurred way back when in China; is probably only really understood by those belonging to each group and is inevitably lessening with time and the impact on both of the outside world.

The Taoism the Yao Mien practice is heavily laced with Shamanism something of which we had witnessed while living in Vietnam. It involves sacrifice of live chickens, a deal of pigs blood, drums, bells, symbolic cut paper figures and people, both men and women, entering a trance in which they speak in voices and have contact with the ancestors. Such mysteries are always conducted with secrecy and are conducive to isolating clan members from all outsiders.

The Yao, along with the Hmong have all these traditions, customs and culture, but still no country of their own. When it became apparent that the Americans were not going to keep their enticing wartime promise of separate Homelands for the Yao and the Hmong and that they would in fact be left to the mercies or otherwise of the general Lao population large numbers of these groups navigated the dangerous waters of the Mekong arriving on the Thai side of the river with just the clothes they stood up in. Here they were housed in refugee camps and with assistance from the United Nations were sponsored, mostly to the USA but also to Canada and

Australia. In this way the Yao nation was splintered yet again and spread thin across an alien lifestyle in a world which each year changes faster than ever and has little inclination toward cultural complexities.

***

Late that afternoon the rainclouds billow away across the surrounding peaks and Mr. Khong keeps his promise to pour the first concrete pylon. A temporary and very fragile-looking scaffolding has been erected and his son, Mr. Kone clambers to the top of it while the rest of the crew form a line from the grinding cement mixer. Small pails of cement pass hand to hand, finally up to Mr. Kone who already knows enough about these odd *falang* to pause dramatically for Iain's camera before tipping the first load into the pylon's formwork. It's a big moment. The two of us cheer and clap. The work-crew smile.

Mr. Kone you will recall is Mr. Khong's son, husband of Bounlee and father of Jarrah. He is a teacher at the government Secondary School at Khoktum, a

Pouring of the first pylon

village fifteen kilometres away at the bottom of the descent from the hills, where there is also the area's small clinic. He would prefer to work full-time at his profession but needs must and when you don't get paid for a couple of months your financial obligations becoming increasingly pressing, especially when you have a small baby. There needs to be a close reassessment by the Lao Government of how the small amount of monies available to it get distributed more equitably. But that is way outside our jurisdiction or even our ability to make an impact. Best to stick with filming Teacher Kone tipping concrete into the pylon's formwork.

We are due another LPB break. Mr. Khong assures us that by the time we return in a few days time all twenty-one pylons will have been poured. All this has happened in a week.

6
HOUSEKEEPING

It was a grand feeling to know that when you came down out of the hills at the close of another physically exhausting day you were leaving the crew in the kind and capable hands of Thongkhanh. He was the best housemother any lad could ever have had.

Within days of the initial land-clearing Thonghkhanh has already been around the traps in the valley and managed to scrounge a dozen or more handmade strips of palm-leaf *attap*. These he and several of the other men attach as extra roofing to the backside of the old schoolhouse covering them with two big blue tarpaulins, both of which are firmly pegged as a precaution against imminent rainy-season storms.

All this meant the school lads loose their dust-bowl petanque court but the girls gain shade where they can challenge each other in complex rope games, a few of them with smaller siblings still slung on their backs. The boys take to spinning hand-made wooden tops or competing with hoops of old tyres.

Girls skip while...

...the boys play with their hand-made tops

All cement bags are stacked on a pallet under the *attap*/tarpaulin ceiling. This tarpaulin continues on down one side and is then carefully tucked underneath the pallets, keeping the bags dry and away from the possibility of wayward hands.

Thonghkhanh is equally meticulous in making sure that a number of pallets, placed in the shade of this roof and raised slightly above the soil, were kept cleared, thus making the crew's dual-purpose eating spot/sleeping space. Nighttime covers were folded and hung over a handmade bamboo rack during the day, along with tee shirts or trousers hand-washed in the river. In an attempt to defeat small nighttime four-footed predators, food is stored in plastic bags tied tight at the neck and slung from the bamboo pole rafters. When serving a meal a piece of cloth is laid on top of the pallets to catch any stray food that is quickly devoured by the numerous dogs. The men always rinse their hands before squatting down to eat and throughout the days they drink copious amounts of water from large plastic containers delivered to the site. Everyone rises before dawn and lays down in the dark, often after a final cigarette and very occasionally a bottle of Beer Lao.

Thongkhanh has brought his handmade fishing nets with him from NaLin. Late in the afternoons, when he goes for his wash in the small stream on the edge of Phoujong village he throws one of these traditional nets in the hope of catching some extra protein for the evening meal.

The tiny fish he traps this way he often put aside to barbecue for us on a stick of split bamboo because he knows we are not up to eating the raw pig, chicken and occasional buffalo meat the workmen enjoy. He gets a fire going in a heartbeat and over this he at first lightly sears some chili that he then pounds into a paste with garlic and whatever other wild herbs he has picked in the forest before stirring it into the finely chopped flesh to make the ubiquitous *laap*. There is always a sufficient quantity of sticky rice available with which the crew can scoop up their meal. This rice, the versatile staple of all Lao meals, which sticks to itself not to the fingers, makes eating utensils non-essential. Its description as a glutinous grain is somewhat misleading, as it contains no gluten, though it is packed with sugar. Thongkhanh always has to hand a wrapped bag of it that he has pre-steamed in a container he has dexterously woven from strips of split bamboo.

Thongkhanh cooking

He is the style of man you'd like to have beside you if the going got tough, a man of many parts and on one of our many bus trips up and down Route 12 Chanthy entertains us with his childhood memories of going on hunting expeditions with his Father to catch much needed food for the struggling Sisombuth family. 'We would go out into the paddy in the dark, with torches tied to our heads. If these lit up two eyes I knew it was a frog and

98

it was safe to grab it. But sometimes the torchlight illuminated only one eye and then I couldn't be sure whether it was a frog, sitting side-on, or a snake and I just had to hope for the best. Of course snakes and frogs are both edible. But...'

Chanthy is wiry and has a deceptive strength, along with a big smile and an infectious warm laugh. 'In the dry season when there were no frogs my Father and I would dig for rats. My Father would lie down and press his ear to the ground listening for the sound of the rats moving about. Once he was sure where they were we would dig in the soil exposing the mouth of their burrows. Then because my hands were so much smaller I would have to quickly force my hand into the dark and drag out a rat. They fought hard and could give you a nasty bite if you weren't quick to hit out their two big front teeth.'

We all laugh but it is impossible not to have a mental flash of our own two children at that age on the beach with their paddle-pops.

On another occasion while waiting roadside in Muang Nan to flag down yet another lumbering public bus, Chanthy is drawn by the sight of a battered motorbike a few metres further down the road that has an openwork wire cage fixed above the front wheel. Inside there is a quartet of rodents, the size of small Australian domestic cats. They look half-dead from heat exhaustion though one still scrabbles wildly in the air when the driver drags it out by the scruff of its neck to give Chanthy a closer look. Its front teeth had been brutally removed. Negotiations are obviously underway.

After a shake of his head Chanthy comes back to where we are standing beside our small packs and with a slightly sheepish look informs us; 'I would like to take that one back to Luang Prabang.'

I say nothing.

Iain asks 'How? Why?'

'In a sack. I want to eat it.'

'In your room? You will kill it, skin it and de-gut it? Then cook it and eat it?' Iain inquires.

Chanthy chews his lower lip. 'I will take it to my cousin. She will know how to do it.'

This being the same cousin who runs the Unexploded Ordnance Museum that sells my calendars.

'If you want so badly to eat that animal then you should kill it yourself,' I comment in prissy tones.

'The man wants only 15,000kip .' (About two dollars)

Neither of us says any more.

Chanthy returns to the hunter, who looks pretty desperate and as if he and the scrawny girl-child with him could do with a meal of rodent themselves. He again holds up the battered creature. Chanthy shakes his head; the man looks crestfallen though with no animosity, the bus clatters down the road and we all board. During the journey that day our three-way conversation is about killing, dying, death and Buddhism as well as 'want' and 'need'; in the Lao language there is tellingly only one word for both those two human emotions.

These bus trips were something I both dreaded and enjoyed. The dread arose from the state of the road, even though it had been much improved since we had first travelled it more than five years previously, there were still wash-aways, landslips, large potholes and chunks of greenery that suddenly manifested themselves. But by far the most frightening aspect of driving this particular route is that it wound its way through villages of wooden shacks on stilts that were oh-so-close to the track of the vehicles that we often came within a whisker of scuttling a too-small child carrying a woven head-strap basket filled with firewood or pails of water.

All this plus the poor driving skills of the drivers, not so much of the buses, because we never travelled at night which was when bus drivers tend to nod off, but drivers of other vehicles on the road. Having an actual Driving License is very unusual in Laos. Even though it is possible to buy one off the shelf without the bother of a Driving Test, it is not seen as an essential piece of paper. Driving skills are picked up as you go along on an ad hoc basis.

Police personnel are of course aware of this but they too, along with teachers and nurses, are poorly paid and often not paid at all for weeks, even months, at a time. So it is generally accepted that if a police officer flags you down you promptly offer money or if you yourself are running short of the readies you mention the name of your cousin who works in the police force. In a nation of a mere six million people almost everyone has a cousin in the police force. Sometimes the ruse works sometimes it doesn't.

During those early trips I begin to register that each time we either zoomed down or chugged up one particularly steep section of the highway the drivers always tooted their horns at the top and bottom. When I mention this to Chanthy he was only too keen to explain that it was to warn off the dreaded *phi*.

'At the time when this road was being upgraded' he tells us, 'a bus full of passengers slid out of control and went over the edge down into the forest here. Everyone on board was killed so the drivers make their horn to warn away the waiting *phi*.' At each tooting spot there was a small coterie of concrete blessing altars. It was interesting to note how many of them were crowded with believer's joss sticks.

So why did we do this hair-raising travel by public

bus instead of hiring a big SUV in LPB and transporting ourselves in style? Because we were trying very hard to minimize costs and such a vehicle would set us back over A$200 for just a one day return journey.

But there was also another reason, which was that we wanted the people with whom we were working not to view us as just another money-dripping, drive-by, NGO or Foreign Aid Organisation, here today, gone tomorrow with no real connection to community or people. This was not some flagellating attempt at self-congratulatory, feel-good heroics. But we did feel that people in the District Centre and along the whole valley of the Hadsaik River could well be watching us and assessing our motives, Over the previous visits we had managed to go from being weird outsiders, who might have ulterior motives like for instance building a Christian Church, to being accepted for what we were, representatives of other *falang* who wished Laos and her people well and who wanted to do their bit to help.

The enjoyment aspect of the bus travel came from the conversations we invariable had with Chanthy on those bus journeys. There undeniably is something about being shut up inside a moving vehicle, whether it's a ship on a world cruise, an airplane on a long flight, a family car on a school holiday trip or in this case a smelly old bus, that is conducive to revealing the heart's hidden intimacies.

**

For our many long-term stays in Muang Nan we chose the Saylomgnen, which translates, to the rather ambitious Soft Spring Wind. This basic roadside guesthouse is run by the Vi family who turn out to be such dedicated card-players that frequently potential guests, many of them Chinese from over the border and quite obviously on business visits, were left stranded at the front entrance while Chanthy hammered on the door of their room out back to alert them to the possibility of customers.

Without any pre-discussion the three of us shared one room with an attached shower/loo. There was a small table and stool and two single-sized beds with thin mattresses and sheets that were rarely if ever changed for the entire three months of our comings and goings. In the morning market we purchase for Chanthy a three-piece concertinaed, kapok-filled mattress that he unfolded on the floor at the foot of our beds and voila: home base.

To westerners, accustomed to many-roomed privacy these domestic arrangements will sound uncomfortably intimate. But Chanthy doesn't like sleeping solo; too many *phi*. He would not have enjoyed and would not have seen any reason for having a separate room. As it was the routine we developed would have made it superfluous. Having haggled for a lift down the mountain, exhausted by a day chockablock with happenings and heat, we would take it in turns to shower before walking along the highway a short distance to what we came to call Flower Café in honour of its splendid array of red flowering succulents growing in big planters along the outside wall. The menu for us was either vegetables and sticky rice or, if we were organized enough to pre-order in the morning, whole fish and sticky rice. For Chanthy there was meat *laap*. Iain had Beer Lao, Chanthy, Coca-Cola and for me there was coconut juice.

The flower café

We would then walk back to the Saylomgnen, exchanging greetings and news with Muang Naners eating in the comparative cool outside their shop-houses as the giant trucks from China roared by. Young girls skipping rope and lads kicking balls wave and shout *falang, falang*. All of them know we were building a School for Phoujong.

Back in our room I collapse facedown on the bed and fall into a stunned painkiller induced slumber while Iain and Chanthy put all their electronic gear on charge and go through details of the day's costs, receipts and bills, along with plans for the following day that invariably starts with a pre-dawn telephone call from his father, Thongkhanh, already up and at 'em on the building site.

'You don't have to stay in with us oldies,' Iain encourages Chanthy who, having attended High School in Muang Nan knew a myriad people locally, many of whom invited him to join in their socializing. Here he is at twenty-four, having graduated from English Language School and now gone on to study Business Administration at college in Luang Prabang. Obviously a highly motivated hard-worker. He would be a catch for any upwardly mobile Lao lass.

'I want to stay with you,' Chanthy always replies. 'I like to. I don't want to go out with them.'

We were so slow, we didn't pick up on why.

***

Breakfast is always a bowl of steaming *pho,* noodle soup, at the Noi's cafe on the edge of the morning market. Housewives take advantage of the hour of dawn as being the only cool time of day to look through the array of fresh produce. There is no lively haggling. Everyone knows everyone else and many are related. Most are struggling financially and anyway the Lao are not a haggling people. Even the Chinese who operate some of the shops that line the sides of the market seem resigned to this and have given up on their genetic predilection for bargaining.

Over the five years we have been visiting Muang Nan we have seen the number of these shops almost double, along with a change to more sophisticated goods and services being available: electronics and this time even a simple hairdressing salon. All of this is excellent business for Mr. Me who owns the complex. Me also starts his days breakfasting in the Noi's café with a number of his cronies. The body language says it all. He has the money/power, is not a man to tangle with and they are his supplicants.

When he becomes bored with the company of these minions he strides off into the area put aside for parking; mostly motorcycles but also a couple of 4-wheel-drives. Me's is the largest and has windows tinted almost black. Opening the back door of this monster vehicle, he turns the sound system up so loud the whole vehicle vibrates and the entire square fills with distorted Thai pop music. The shopkeepers and small fruit and vegetable stallholders pause only briefly at this embarrassingly macho display before returning to their selling.

There would hardly be one of them who doesn't know that Me's wife and mother of his three, now adult, children had a fling with the Korean man who, a couple of years back, came to oversee the building, of the impressively massive Park Kone bridge across the Mekong a few kilometres further along Route 12. This has necessitated the total resettlement of many hundreds of villagers from Thaduea village, a process that has been disturbing to watch. The bridge completed, the man moved on to his next project. Mr. Me and his wife divorced.

The café-owning Noi's, both of them have the same first name, have four children, two of whom, Mr. Meo and Miss Fone have been born in the years we have been breakfasting in their café. We have watched the oldest, Mr. Mingkee, a boy now sixteen, develop from a gawky pimply-faced kid into a confident young man. He is in his final year of High School but already he also has a job, paid for by Mr. Me. He collects the garbage, mostly plastic and cardboard wrappings, but also materials that are less pleasant to handle, from the marketplace shops and stalls. Behind a small but powerful Chinese built lod-sin, (more about these vehicles to come) Mingkee has attached a tray with home built woven bamboo sides to create a garbage truck. Decked out with a facemask, long plastic gloves and big rubber boots he spends at least an hour every day, before school, confidently driving from shop to shop, piling in their garbage.

A couple of times a week he drives a few kilometres out onto the Hadsaik River Valley Road and dumps all he has collected beside the river, where occasionally it is burnt. What remains, gradually slides down the riverbank and in the annual rainy season flooding is swept away.

Mingkee frequently sits with us after his morning's work and gets himself up to speed with what is happening with the School at Phoujong. He also tells tales to Chanthy about his former alma mater and the teachers whom Chanthy remembers from his days there. Its touching for us to see how apparent it is that Mingkee is a little in awe of Chanthy and his educational and lifestyle achievements. Whereas we view Chanthy from our age perspective as a very young man, Mingkee admires him as a local lad made good and someone to emulate. We can see that Chanthy rather relishes this role.

In between conversations Mingkee takes meal orders, serves customers their food, cleans dishes, all the while keeping an eye on his two youngest siblings who toddle and crawl on the floor among the legs of customers, too close for my comfort to the open fire where Ms. Noi boils, steams and fries her food. Frail but feisty Grandma often picks up the baby and sits her down beside her while she unwraps from a cloth huge amounts of sticky rice and gives it an essential airing before re-wrapping it. The fourth child, ten-year-old Mr. Kome, still at primary school, and not as spontaneously hard-working as his big brother, needs to be chivvied into clearing and wiping tables. By seven o'clock Mingkee takes off on a motorbike for school while laggardly Kome drifts off in the same direction by foot. No one in the family waves or says goodbye, to them a mystifying *falang* habit. Instead and without fuss they weave their way into and through family life.

***

To return to the lod-sin: if indeed this is an accurate transliteration of the name, as even the Internet is silent on this one. With or without the blessing of this information, rapidly increasing numbers of lod-sins have taken over this part of the world, all in the space of six months. On our first visit to NaLin in 2011 we were transported to the village by a tok-tok. Not the ubiquitous tuk-tuk, the open-sided truck that is used in all Lao towns as taxis. But a tok-tok.

The newly-arrived lod-sin, which actually uses the same fly-wheel-enhanced motor as the old tok-tok has, as you can see here two cargo or passenger trays;

The old tok-tok versus...

...the new lod sin

one at the back and one at the front. The driver sits in the middle in a much easier driving position than the awkward, but somehow effective, long handle-bar approach. The overwhelming appeal of the new vehicle, with prices starting at about US$3,000, is reflected in booming sales and in the numbers of them seen on the road. The lod-sin also happens to be a fairly dramatic example of how Chinese technology, in this case, fairly low-level technology, is impacting all of South East Asia.

As we leave the Noi's café I make sure to wave to the young girl with whom I am slowly building a language-free friendship. She is perhaps twelve or thirteen, the same age as our grand-daughter, and this must be her pre-school job because every morning she sits cross-legged on a piece of tarpaulin in the market with her produce neatly arranged before her: pairs of buffalo hooves, complete with ten centimeters or so of butchered hairy leg. They are very hard for me to contemplate. When I ask Chanthy about them he politely tries not to show his surprise that I don't know. 'They make a very good soup base,' he assures me. Obviously they are good sellers because the girl is there every day with new stock to sell before she goes off to school.

Now we must do some housekeeping ourselves in the way of paying the Project's bills. We make a call on big, and I mean big, Mr. Thone who has a minute wife and two small children, one of them a baby still at the breast.

School-girl with her buffalo hooves for sale in Muang Nan market

Mr. Thone has built his family owned and operated business from scratch over the past nine years by getting in on the ground floor of the country's slow but steadily growing building industry. Laos only joined the market economy in 1988 and has barely managed to

112

hang in there through the spill-over effects from the tide of economic woes resulting from the 2008 world-wide recession created by greedy people in countries he knows little about and understands even less.

A few days back a gang of us, including Mr. Khong, Thongkhanh, several of the tradies from the Project and the three of us had paid an evening visit to the storage facility, adjoining Mr Thone's brick-built family house, facing onto Highway 12 on the edge of town. Mr. Thone, woken from a nap by his delicate wife, had come out still putting on his shirt, to discuss reinforcing rods, metal roofing sheets and cement, all of which he imports from either Thailand or VietNam and gravel and sand dredged from the nearby Mekong River. His small daughter trailed behind us on a tricycle decorated with Angry Bird stickers. Mr. Khong and Thongkhanh inspected the quality of the goods, drove the bargains and arranged for materials to be delivered. It is likely that Mr. Khone has never been up into the mountains as far as Phoujong because after dropping off the first load of cement and sand he told us that unfortunately he had under-quoted and due to the condition of the road, from now on he would have to charge 15,000 kip ($2) extra for each trip in order to cover transport costs.

There was no way we were going to argue with him over that. It was tough enough travelling up in a Hyundai tray-back, but the wear and tear on the tyres alone, plus the strain on the engine, of a cement or sand and gravel laden ten-tonne truck certainly warranted that bit extra.

We pay for the first of the deliveries that have already been made and it is not Mr. Thone who takes the stacks of kip but his tiny wife. She flicks expertly, backwards, through the bundles, baby in a front sling, toddler still attached to tricycle, writes us a receipt and goes inside to stash the payment in their safe.

Next it is the timber merchant's shop-house a little further into town but also on the highway. Again the same routine. The bundles of kip quickly and precisely counted, backwards, by the wife of the timber merchant, a receipt given and this time the word Phoujong and the universal thumbs up sign for approval. Throughout all of this it is a couple of primary school-aged daughters hang close-by to watch proceedings, while the merchant himself continues to load his truck with planks he and his co-workers have sawn from trees they have felled in nearby plantations the family owns.

Teak plantations are everywhere, especially in mountainous areas but a large proportion of this crop is sold into overseas markets, predominately next-door neighbour China. Teak trees are still seen as a family's hedge against future financial demands; a wedding, a funeral or illness, and families try to hold on to them until they reach their potential maximum size. Increasingly plantations of teak have been planted and managed by large agri-businesses, again owned by China.

After this there is a payment to be made for cement blocks made at a small, again family-owned and operated, factory on the opposite side of town. Again it is the wife who collects, counts backwards and stashes the cash payment and gives the receipt.

We feel it is as important to pay these bills promptly as it is to pay the building crew regularly.

Throughout all these kip settlements Chanthy's mobile runs hot mostly with requests from his Father for other necessities to be bought and sent up on whatever vehicle he can persuade to make the trip. Nails, String. Hosepipe. Always water and, please, from our personal funds, some nappies for baby Jarrah.

7 BACKSTORY

There is also housekeeping to be attended to in Luang Prabang. During our intermittent stays for this Project in the former Royal Capital we had been house-sharing for minimal rent with Michael McLaggan. A thirty-something American philosopher, Michael's lifestyle pleasingly contrasted with ours. He was writing both an esoteric novel and a full-on philosophical treatise which he was due to present at a gathering of top-grade philosophers due to be held later in the year in India. Michael is a night owl and like his feathered namesake he captures his most mouth-watering, in his case, intellectual, morsels in the deepest dark of night, whereas we are members of the early-to-bed-early-to-rise species.

We are granted only rare sightings of Michael's spectral figure, with its long black beard, in its long black coat topped by a black homburg, when we come across him at the outside garden table blinking in unaccustomed daylight, trapped at his writing place on his computer, by some thought that has kept him alert all night. We wave as we wheel our bicycles past him to take off on our early morning cycle beside the Mekong River. He loosely acknowledges us, blinded as he is by some tantalizingly elusive idea.

The house is rented by fellow-Australians John and Robyn Salisbury who spend half the year working as a builder and hairdresser in the hinterland of Queensland's Gold Coast and the other half working with their heart-son Bounmee and his wife Nou running the Apple Guest House in Luang Prabang's upmarket downtown accommodation area that is replete with scores of *wats*. Bounmee himself spent his childhood living in a village *wat* in the north of the country before taking up the Salisbury's generous offer of a home and education in Australia where he studied to become a licensed builder. The four of them now own and operate the Apple Guest House, that they renovated themselves and have a seemingly unending store of Fawlty Towers-type tales that bring tears of laughter to the eyes.

John and Robyn are presently in Australia but due home at month's end. Philosopher Michael has been looking after the place for them until their return and, though they have offered for us to also stay on in the house after their return, we're sure that it would be something of a stretch bathroom and loo-wise. Added to which, the five kilometre morning cycle in from the somewhat outlying area of Vieng Mai village, though beneficial for our mental and physical health, is becoming an increasingly sweaty experience in the all too familiar annual rise of heat and humidity.

The final decision to move into the heart of town is made on the morning when the electricity suddenly fails. When Iain returns from unshackling the bikes from the side fence it is to tell me that a large-scale clearance has begun of the wooden shanties lining the track up to the house. In the process an excavator has sliced through buried cabling and this has left the entire neighbourhood powerless. No electricity means no way to use our computers to download footage already shot of the School Project and no way to stay in touch via telephone over what is needed on site or even to charge our cameras and send and receive emails. But also, first things first, because the house has an electrically operated water supply, it means no shower and no loo.

Closer inspection reveals that our own small community of homes is in distinct peril of slipping down the gash that has been torn into the hillside. It would appear that no advance warning of this demolition had been given to owners of the small homes built around us, in order that they could be somewhat prepared. That's just the way things happen and the villagers are resigned to having to wait until 'someone' fixes the cascade of problems. Among the chatter of acceptance we hear frequent repetition of the same well-worn Lao phrase. *Bo peng yang.* No worries. Depending on your state of mind and the situation you find yourself in this phrase ranges in impact from amusing to mildly irritating through to downright exasperating.

At six am it is already too hot to consider exasperation. Instead we accept the villagers help to manhandle our hired bikes down off the precipice of mud, and across the rapidly expanding and deepening lake of slippery mud to push out of the laneway past the corner funeral parlour and onto the busy main road. Here we begin the cycle into town for a restorative coffee at our favourite riverside restaurant.

From previous experiences in Laos we know that there is no second-guessing how long it will take to fix Vieng Mai's water problems. The one thing we do however know for sure is that we are under considerable time-restraints due to the ever-present imminence of the annual rains. We need to keep the pedal to the metal. There is no leeway for *bo peng yang.* We decide to scope out other rental possibilities within Luang Prabang there and then.

Unfortunately we are now confronted with

another, what could turn out to be an even larger, problem: Chinese New Year. It is all but upon us. Our northern neighbours are surging across the border. Still we decide to bite the bullet and its just as well we do because the powers-that-be take almost a week to mop up Vieng Mai's excess water and to get power back to the neighbourhood. By then the backlog of orders for delicate balsawood coffins decorated with intricate gold and white paper cutout designs must have been stupendous. Some businesses are guaranteed to never run short of customers.

***

We have welcomed in Chinese New Year in many places around the globe across the years. Every time we have been amazed by its increasing muscularity and size. Last year in Luang Prabang I remember both of us saying to the other, surely it can't get any bigger than this. This year's impact proves us wrong yet again.

For the past few such occasions we have ceased to be amazed by the sheer numbers of Chinese visitors from neighbouring southern provinces of China...nearly all of them coming by road. Their increase without seeming end is now just an accepted matter of fact. Like sunrise and sunset. What stupefies now is the social changes the celebrations represent.

Last year Luang Prabang was so unprepared for the onslaught of numbers that the town literally ran out of noodles. True. Hard to believe, but true.

Our early morning habits I have mentioned previously usually mean that we get breakfast done and dusted while the majority are still musing about the day ahead. So we had been truly shocked to discover on the second, or maybe the third, day of the holiday that by 7am the market, the sidewalk food stalls, the cafes and the restaurants, the whole kit and caboodle, had run out of noodles.

Even the Lao recipe of *bo peng yang* offered no solace to Government office workers and shop assistants whose daily heart-starter bowl of *pho* was, without warning, unavailable. There were mutterings. Marie Antoinette's infamous remark about 'let them eat cake' paled by comparison. For a people accustomed to stringencies brought about by Government policies this loss of a daily staple, gorged almost pre-dawn by their fellow-Communists, proved a bridge too far. This year Central Planning, or at least the noodle-making ladies in the shops down the road, were better prepared and there was no lack of noodles.

No, this year the biggest impact was one not of quantity but of quality. Regular family Chinese made sedans still came in large numbers crossing the border of Laos and Yunnan Province at Boten. But whereas they had previously travelled in convoys, headlights on, horns blaring and flying national flags, as they snaked their non-stop way through town, this year there is very apparent increase in the number of high-end model sedans, many of them of quality make foreign brands such as Audi, BMW and Mercedes. They travel as individual vehicles, often-large SUV versions with darkened windows. The people who step out from their mostly leather seats are well dressed, in fact somewhat over-dressed. And there are sizeable numbers of those, oh dear, obstreperous little beasts that have resulted from China's one-child policy. Loudly spoilt Princesses and Princes. They eat in the more expensive restaurants where these little darlings are given the sort of full-rein up to now usually associated with *falang* members of a different culture.

As die-hard campers, the vehicles that most impress us are the extremely up-market four-wheel-drive versions replete with state of the art kitchens and ablution facilities, plus comfortable beds, air-con, satellite TV, solar power, retractable awnings, sat/nav and large scale maps drawn on their sides showing where the owners have travelled.

It was these people whose extended visits we most noticed because, to do the travelling they were engaged in required money, maturity, interest and leisure time and more importantly, the confidence and desire to really get out in the world and have a look for themselves. These were no 'I've done Laos' drop-ins.

Age may remove agility, dammit, but coincidentally it improves long-term perspective and we well recall how it was several decades before the post war economic boom in Japan encouraged real-on-the-ground individual travelers. Good financial times, for some, in India does not seem to have created a blossoming of confident independent travelers. I have yet to see camper-travelers from the sub-continent. You may gather from all this that while highly trained economists have their own academically legitimized way of assessing how well a nation is doing, I have another rather more subterranean method; but one I am convinced is just as accurate, if not more so. People traveling solo, especially young women traveling solo, are a sure sign that a nation's economy is booming and as this year we saw a big upsurge in this style of person my China Economy Index would assess that there is a tidal wave of wealth yet to run out of puff in the Central Kingdom.

It is when we are on the brink of running out of puff ourselves that we at last find accommodation that literally suits our bill. We had started off by dropping by our friends at Khoum Xieng Thong Guest

House, where we've stayed in previous years, but Noi and Thiemchanh were all Chinesed out. From there we had cycled our way along the waterfronts of both rivers, the Mekong and the Nam Canh looking for a simple room that fit our requirements; air-conditioning, space to set up our computer gear plus beauty. That last one is always the most difficult to fulfill but it is also the top of our list because dilettante though it may initially sound, beauty is what nourishes life. In the end it is our national background, plus the fact that we want a place for a couple of months and are happy to pay up-front, cash, that brought us to Mekong Charm. Here, with a balcony where we can work, overlooking the mighty river, we meet Taykeo Sayavongkhamdy who, having had all four of her now adult children complete their tertiary education in Australia on scholarships, is inclined to feel favourably towards citizens of the Great Southern Land. Over the next little while we come to know Taykeo and even to meet her family but for now the immediate need is to set up our electricity deprived equipment and be in touch with the other world.

***

While Iain downloads and uploads and makes shot lists and tries to plan ahead visually as well as keeping the accounts up to date I write emails to Project Supporters. We think it is an absolute necessity to do this because without supporters there would be no Project. We owe it to each one of them to keep them in touch and up to date with what is happening. We don't want to simply take their money and run. I know all this could be written as an update on Facebook, a blog or a web page. But there you go. Mass communication is not my style. I feel happier one on one. There are now over one hundred of these ones. Each is an individual who for singular reasons has put their hand in their pocket and helped make all this happen. They deserve at least the recognition that a one-on-one email, with photographs, can bring.

When we had, at first unknowingly, started almost six years ago, on this course in life we had no idea of how or where to begin. We just saw the need and felt compelled to try to fulfill it. It just seemed so obvious. We had not been looking for other deeper motives and were already embarked on other roads. Our lives were filled to the brim with other desires but all of these simply fell away. It was as if we had been gifted with a challenge that we could not refuse.

The Road to NaLin side-swiped us into new and sometimes not very comfortable spaces. Selling the idea to others, raising the more than $30 thousand we tentatively estimated it would take to build an all-weather road into, through and out of Chanthy's village, obtaining permits to create a legal Charity Fund in Australia, deciphering road engineering requirements, learning the language of all these aspects of these ideas, it all took time; time in very large amounts. It meant learning life-lessons late in life. It meant testing bonds of family and friendships. It required pushing ourselves physically and mentally and finding out whether or not we could come up to the mark. Of course it was fun, but there were quite a few times when it didn't feel like fun!

What did we know about building a road? Zilch. What did we know about putting in culvert drains? Also zilch. In fact up to the time we built sixteen of them I hadn't even registered what the word culvert described. And creating a school? Ditto.

We just had this extraordinarily naïve idea that having managed, more by good luck than by good planning, to reach our biblically allotted lifespan we must by now surely know enough people whom we could interest in these schemes and whose financial trust in us we could repay while at the same time improving the lives of our friends in the Hadsaik Valley, who also grew to believe in us to a touching degree.

The big breakthrough as we rode the emotional roller coaster of raising funds for the building of The Road came when Pip and Dick Smith, whom we have known on a casual basis for some decades, donated two massive hits, the first of $5000 and the second of

$10,000 towards The Road and the culvert drains, followed by a further $5,000 for The School. When we apologetically informed Dick that although our Fund was registered as a charitable body, we had not jumped through the fiery hoops of establishing it as a tax concession, he told us that he and Pip rarely donated monies to charities that were tax deductible. All they required was a simple receipt. We have been eating Dick Smith Peanut Butter ever since!

Dick & Pip Smith

We did not start out with the idea of pulling together a documentary. Nor did I intend to write a book. Sorry to say, but there was no plan! What happened just grew into being. When the showing of Iain's independently shot documentary at our local art-house cinema, Cinemax, owned by friends Stephen and Deborah Bugé, brought people out of the woodwork who asked, yes actually asked, to make donations, well what could we do but put in the all important culverts. Culverts by then I had learnt were huge drains used to channel the heavy monsoon rains away from the all-weather track. The only previous time I had registered these essential pieces of road engineering was in India where people at almost the bottom of the economic ladder, use them as temporary housing. But now of course I see them everywhere, most especially on the oh-so-slow to be built and surely jokingly referred to Pacific Highway.

The documentary was also shown at the Bowls Club at the nearby coastal village of Cabarita, an event organised by our friend Michelle Townsend. On both these occasions we held auctions and raffles and sold door prizes. More lessons for us in how to open people's hearts and purses. We also spread the word about the Projects and made new contacts.

After the building of the culverts (there's that word again) I finished the writing of my book on both Projects and while Iain made a second documentary I also put together three 2015 calendars, Village Ceremony, Village People and Village Life. Books and calendars were on sale at the documentary showing, again at the Cabarita Bowls Club and at Kingscliff Cinemax,

The highlight of the screening at Kingscliff was the supporting auction of three Aboriginal paintings, by well-known Central Desert artists, from the collection of good friend Alan Wilson. Alan, previously a theatre and television actor who also later ran a successful theatrical agency, made the link between the very disadvantaged minority people of Laos and the Aboriginal people of Australia whose work he collects.

Alan Wilson and Stephen Bugé pour champagne before the screening at Kingscliff Cinemax

With a few pertinent, heartfelt remarks, he focused the minds of everyone in the audience on the universal need for understanding and sharing, while raising $1500 towards building a School for Phoujong.

A few weeks later we held our biggest and most successful publicity achievement so far, at the TAFE College of Education at Randwick in Sydney.

On this evening, which was the brainchild and heart-work of tireless TAFE teacher and administrator Janet Brennand, we showed both documentaries, sold calendars and books as well as running an auction and raffles alongside selling tickets for door prizes. Janet, her husband Dick Sheppard, their daughters Hannah and Megan, together with a coterie of their mates made and served delicious dhal and rice plus herbal teas for close to 100 people.

The atmosphere was extraordinarily positive with friends from various stages and places in our lives from the Himalaya and the Sahara to former colleagues at the ABC

Hannah, Megan, Dick & Janet

and commercial television channels reaching into their pockets with such generosity that we raised $7000 on that one night.

It was an emotional evening for us on many levels. Meeting old friends such as Astrophysicist Richard Hunstead and his professional gardener-extraordinaire wife Penny, along with Everest summiteer Greg Mortimer and his fellow Antarctic adventurer wife Margaret Werner. There was also an unplanned meeting-up for the first time face to face with Sid and Margaret French people who didn't know us from a bar of soap and yet who out of the blue had sent us $5000 for our first Road project.

Two days later, because of an introduction by our very longtime friend Jan Cristaudo, we were approached by Michael Symons, who with his Swedish wife Mimi, has single-handedly established the independent aid group, Cobra and Mongoose

cobra&
mongoose

OUR PROJECTS
TAKE A DETAILED LOOK

(please check out their website). Jan was having an exhibition of her abstract art at a gallery that was formerly the Walter Burley Griffin Incinerator in the Sydney suburb of Willougby. She held a silent auction at the exhibition that raised $12,000 and donated this to Cobra and Mongoose. We had never met Michael but having heard of our work he had recently visited the villages of NaLin and Phoujong, accompanied by his seventeen-year-old son Carl. Carl had never before travelled beyond the surfing beaches of Sydney. There the two of them saw the dire need in both places and Michael offered $9000 to the growing Project that we were currently estimating would cost around $30,000. Wheels within wheels.

***

So here we were, back again with our ever-expanding circle of Lao friends but most importantly with our special Lao friend Chanthy Sisombuth: our Buddhist mentor and cultural guide from whom we have learnt so much.

Across these years he has supported himself, as well as putting in to the demands of the ever-expanding family finances. He began by labouring on building sites but for such physically demanding work and long hours the pay was ridiculously low. He next worked   as a waiter at a riverside restaurant, which is how we met him, then as a sales assistant in an up-market French-owned Lao arts and crafts shop and on into his present job with a rapidly expanding independent tourist operator. He lives in a small rented room that at least, unlike his first place, has its own indoor toilet and shower. With no request from him we help him financially with his accommodation and education to a far lesser extent than the majority of middle-income Australian mums and dads put out for their teenaged children's pocket money.

Chanthy's days start before dawn when he fires up his rice cooker and goes to the nearby local market for his daily food requirements. When you have no fridge you need to shop daily. There are frequent religious observances at the local *wat* he attends. Invariably he then calls to have a chat with his Mother or Father and by 7am he is at the travel office in Luang Prabang's main street. Here he uses his constantly expanding mastery of English together with his good manners and warm personality to cold-sell tours face to face to *falang* who come in off the street. I have surreptitiously watched him, with pride and amusement, as he goes through this ritual. Always I am amazed at how he answers what are to me preposterous questions (will it be hot?) politely explaining that he is unable to bargain over the fixed prices because he is merely an employee. At the same time he suggests that they compare his prices with those of other tours on offer so they can see what good value he is offering. He always proffers his personalized business card, carefully pointing out his telephone number, while assuring the visitor that he is available 24/7. His competence makes people feel safe while at the same time arousing their sense of adventure.

Tourism in Laos is the invariable twin-edged sword that it is in any poor country. It operates at the whim and fancy of over-indulged visitors, so jaded they tire quickly of every new destination and are always looking for the latest quirky fad. It's a tart's game. I recall a comment made by one blighted soul who informed us with a degree of hauteur that she and her husband 'never did the same country twice.'

So I think that for your heart's sake you have to get in and out as quickly as possible while milking it for all it is worth. In Chanthy's case, a degree in Business Administration and in the case of his boss, a few more steps up the rickety bamboo ladder of the overall Laotian economy.

By eleven Chanthy leaves the office to ride a cousin's motorbike to college that is fortunately close by in compact Luang Prabang. Here he attends classes until four in the afternoon after which he returns to the world of travel for several more hours. In the high and cooler season of the dry, from late October through to March the main street is still abuzz with potential customers until well after nine pm. Then there are homework studies to be done.

Eating and such domestic demands as the washing of clothes have to be fitted in where possible. Life goes on at this pace for the entire college year. And then there are the elephants.

Chanthy's boss, a man from southern Laos, is set on growing his business as fast and furiously as he can. It makes us nervous, because we can imagine how overstretched he is at the banks and other less reputable loan institutions, including, no doubt, family. His empire has the feel of one of those card trick houses magicians can throw up for delighted audiences who then watch it all collapse.

In the past year he has expanded by opening several new branch offices of his main business. The biggest one has a coffee shop attached at which staff are pressured into encouraging indecisive visitors to sit and peruse the surfeit of colour brochures advertising the company's produce, while drinking cups of expensive, though good, Lao coffee.

Because of the long work hours, constant surveillance by the boss checking on personal mobile phone calls, constraining breaks for quick meals and demands to perform jobs outside of those required for original employment, the staff turnover is constant. In fact during the three months we were in Laos this time several newly employed men and women did one day's work and never returned. For them it was also probably the elephants.

'The boss', Chanthy informs us one morning, with a quiver in his voice, 'wants me to go out to his river camp and work with the elephants.' Chanthy is not a wimp. Though small in build, he is wiry and strong and as a village lad he is willing and able to take on a multitude of unexpected tasks. But elephants are big. Very big. As well as being far from docile. They have minds of their own. And emotions that it takes a professional mahout a lifetime with which to bond.

The river camp that Chanthy was referring to is only a few kilometres from the centre of town and is the site chosen by the boss on which to start up his latest expansionary investment, a forest lodge. Visitors stay overnight in simple cabins that have balcony views across the wide shallows. They ride the huge beasts, helping to wash and scrub them down in the waters, feed them and in general get up close and friendly. It's a great experience. We have done it ourselves, when our daughter Zara and her husband Jay visited from San Francisco, where they live ...although at a different camp

Zara and Jay with the elephants

This particular camp, owned and operated by a German who has lived in Laos for decades, does excellent work, rehabilitating elephants who have been overworked in the country's north-western forests; sometimes even fed drugs to keep them working long after they would naturally rest. A really terrific annual Elephant Festival has been established; also in the north east, and we spent several days there one year, along with seemingly half the population of Laos and a similar number of Thais. The idea behind this festival is to improve people's knowledge of these animals and to hopefully increase their respect for them.

All we could suggest to Chanthy was that he went out to the camp to see what was required of him and then judge whether or not he felt comfortable with this expansion in his work-duties.

'Its all right' he tells us with a relieved smile over a meal, necessarily eaten quickly, that evening. 'I just feed them. Many bananas and much special grass.' We joke about how much these animals eat. 'They also make big toilet, ' Chanthy assures us, 'that I have to clean away.'

I have been trying to think of an equivalent request from a boss in Australia. Perhaps something like being employed as an IT expert then being suddenly informed that you are also required to clean the outside of the office windows while dangling fifty metres about street level in one of those swaying window-cleaning carts that take your breath away.

Within a week Chanthy is also collecting feed by the truck-load from the camp's adjacent forest and as well scrubbing down the giant pachyderms all of which progressed, as we had always known it would, into sitting way up high on the elephants' necks telling tales to wide-eyed innocent tourists. As is his nature Chanthy even started to enjoy his mahout role and in future years all this will add sparkle to his CV..

8 INSULATION

Hi there Zas

Sabaidee! hope all going well in your world.

Here everything is happening so fast...all so jam-packed... that it is hard to keep a handle on it...

But here we are back again in LPB for the wash and brush up act.

We have moved into town...Aussie mates John and Robyn come back tomorrow and apart from being without water for two days...and power for one...(the government are building a road! and an *over enthusiastic front end loader chappie was a trifle too slap-happy and chopped through a water mains! which gushed everywhere...making the soil soggy so the power poles leant over and the wires all came down! not so safe!) But...as I said, apart from that the washing/peeing in the night...would have been a trifle too family friendly with us all at home... so we are now in a guesthouse overlooking the Mekong...from whose balcony early this am I spotted Batman in full kit! And watched a wedding procession...*

Everything with the School building is going apace...so fast and furious in fact that I can't do anything more on site but take pix and try to remain on my feet! No time for planning/ designing/ thinking...so that has to be done here.

The building crew is so fantastically great. Non-stop they go go go and when things are not available they simple improvise! They all cook and make meals together and there is an excellent atmosphere of camaraderie. So impressive. Lots of laughter and smiles all round. The party atmosphere sort of reminds me of Beyond 2000 in the early days before the moneymen moved in.

The kids are of course having a GREAT time. I can't be sure whether I told you about Bounyang last year? The eight year old massively disabled lad...we personally (nothing to do with Project funds) brought him to LPB...to the Chinese hospital where he was diagnosed with polio (probably from birth)... and of course severe anaemia (in common with most of the children in the village)...and malnutrition (ditto)...his prospects looked pretty damn dim...but now he is back home using a walker to get about...his legs are in braces...and what a look on his face...very hard ...in fact impossible...not to be enchanted to tears...but of course that is not to happen! When I look through the pix/video I see him popping up everywhere! Using his walker and getting into life.

Chanthy's Dad is sleeping on site as paid Supervisor...to keep an eye on all the stuff.

We needed a culvert put in to have a small earth bridge built so as to cross the stream with the big trucks bringing the sand/gravel/cement/iron...

As with all good stories there has of course been a wee bit of jeopardy! To be expected...after all this is a village of mixed ethnicities...with long histories of edginess...but nothing Iain can't schmooze his way through!

Overall...there is a palpable feeling of positive energy in the country, many changes developments ... just in the small area we cover in our travel and chats. Its infectious and we are both bubbling with ideas!

This weekend we have to finalize designs of desks/benches/shutters...as these are being made by Sengchan...the former Pathet Lao soldier in NaLin... and he needs to start on them...logistics and all.

We also need yet more thinking/talking about loos...

Maintenance has not been a priority so far in the life of Phoujong or the school...they were only just managing to keep their noses above the waterline... but as this building becomes what we plan for it to be...a baseline...a watershed...then all this changes... and there needs to be discussions about its future uses and how to make these work and keep working...

Before the villagers were a bunch of uprooted transplanted people...now this building is giving focus/hope...and a future that requires maintenance!

The foundations have been dug...the support pillars are all in place. Soon the slab/s.

We have the word that electricity will happen in the next two years or so....So we are planning for that...wiring/fans/switches etc.

We have a commitment from and contract with the builder...Khong...who is Chanthy's sister's Bounlee's father in law...and so Jarrah's granddad and delighted with his first grandchild and loves the name...

Khong's daughter Zon...has become 'engaged' ... so of course there was a massive village street baci ceremony...and Chanthy saved us from a terrible blunder...I wanted to buy a basket of fruit etc wrapped in cellophane...but were told just in time that it was in fact a gift to take to a funeral!!! Oops!

We have also been given the go ahead and signed papers with the Education Department...no kickbacks... all we did was take them all to lunch!...

A new paediatric hosp. has been opened in LPB... built by a terrific Japanese philanthropist.....oddly enough I had been thinking of approaching him! So if you know of anyone medical who wants to volunteer..............here's their opportunity.

Now I must go...strike a blow etc...with the shots/ footage/expenses...before the overwhelming need to have some mid morning shuteye seizes me!

We both find we work in four hour hits....with necessary breaks in between...early mornings are best...before the heat clamps in...

Sorry if this is all too much to grasp! But there you go.

LOVE and HUGS...

Give everyone you see a hug from me...why not! Chanthy has a tee-shirt bearing the slogan...Free Hugs Baby....he was embarrassed when we told him what it meant! but we said...go for it!

mum oxox

You may be able to tell from the edgy tone of this catch-up email to our daughter in San Francisco that by now we were living on adrenalin spiced up with a ferocious dose of the crazies!

We had been in LPB for three days though constantly in touch through Chanthy's mobile with his Father on the building site and we were now hanging out to get back there because Thongkhanh told us the formwork for the walls was going up at a pace.

It is Nalin Headman Dith who picks us up from our Muang Nan guesthouse in his rattletrap Hyundai to make the journey up the mountain. Dith has his ever-smiling wife Thone with him and also his shy sixteen-year-old daughter Nit. While we each have a bowl of *pho* in Mr. and Mrs. Noi's market café to sustain us through the day ahead, Nit's plans for her future come up for discussion. She is in her last year at high school and from the conversation it appears she wants to go on to study to become a nurse.

NaLin Headman, Mr. Dith, his wife Thone and daughter Nit.

I think this is brilliant. Laos is in dire need of a decent medical set-up. If you have anything even only a little worse than a common cold, and if you can afford to, you go across the border to Thailand to seek medical help. Here is a girl on the brink of womanhood who is keen to pursue a career as a nurse: a job that would open to her the wider world of independence and the self-esteem this would bring, that would vault her out of the village restraints of poverty and dependence.

So I enthuse about her plan and begin asking where she could train and how much it would cost. Both her mum and dad also appear keen on the idea. All this you must remember is taking place through the translation of Chanthy who immediately put a damper on the scheme by saying she should instead become a teacher.

Although Laos needs teachers too because, lets face it Laos is in need of everything, if nursing was what most appealed to Nit then, I think, she should be encouraged to follow her heart. I say as much.

Chanthy shakes his head before enlarging on his thinking. 'There are so few hospitals in Laos that jobs for nurses are very hard to find, though it is true that if you do get a job you are more likely to be paid regularly because there is a big need for nurses. Whereas,' he goes on, 'for teachers there has been a continuing increase in schools being built and jobs are therefore more available, though you are less likely to get paid regularly because there are a lot of teachers to fill the jobs. It is better for Ms. Nit and her family that she trains as a teacher. I can help get her a place at the Teacher's Training College in Luang Prabang, where I studied English, because I know people who teach there. It also costs less to train as a teacher.'

So, there you go, that's the sad conundrum facing this bright, committed young woman from the very start of her adult life: train in a profession which has less personal appeal for the reason that when you graduate you will be able to find employment even though your salary payment will be irregular; or take up the inspirational life role that that you most desire but in which it will be more difficult to find regular paid employment.

Poverty and its attached inequalities are surely a matter of fate. It will cost US$1000 a year, for three years, to put Nit through her nursing training.

After that conversation we are all somewhat subdued as Mr. Dith struggles with the wheel that tosses him and us about this way and that, while he negotiates the last few kilometres of the track into Phoujong.

But it is worth every bruising bone-jarring jolt for

as we drive across the culvert and grind the gears to get up the steep slope on the far side a School for Phoujong comes into view and Iain and I shout aloud and laugh hugely with joy.

Of course not the completed School for Phoujong, far from that, but enough of the concrete blockwork for the walls, windows, doorways and even roof-shape are in place so that the bare bones skeleton of the building presents itself rising like perhaps a miracle would appear, from the bare soil.

Ready for the roofing

Iain and I tumble out of the truck before it has fully stopped and run towards it, arms out, making w h o o p i n g laughing sounds. We clutch each other's hands and then to the amazed embarrassment of everyone else, we hug each other and I am sorry to have to admit, get a bit teary!

Of course we pull ourselves together pretty smartish and try to excuse ourselves for, by Lao standards, such an outlandish display of emotion, but the whole lot of them continue laughing at our behaviour and everyone shakes hands with everyone else and smiles broadly. Because lets face it what has been achieved, even just this far, is so totally outrageous!

It is another tipping point.

Seeing our display of happiness over the building of the School gives everyone a glimpse into how important this Project is to us. Perhaps for the first time over the years, road, culverts and now school, the villagers realise we care at a very deep level for what is being achieved; that the School is personal to us: a part of our lives.

For a quarter of an hour Builder Khong and Site Supervisor Thongkhanh take us on an up close and personal examination in detail of what has been built and they talk about what materials are needed for the next big moves.

The time has come to tell them of our passionate secret; something we had kept to ourselves until now because we feared immediate rejection. That fear is based on the knowledge that what we wanted to suggest, no, more than suggest, gently insist on, would be an unknown to them and therefore would more than likely be shunned without further consideration. Almost everyone around the world is secretly, or otherwise, afraid of new ideas.

We had spoken to Chanthy about this idea and made it clear to him that he should keep it to himself until the time was ripe. It could get no riper because the first roof beams had already been placed in position so we could wait no longer. We sense that Chanthy also thinks there will be opposition to our idea and in fact that he does not go for it one hundred percent himself.

In common with every other day it is extremely hot on site so Iain suggests that we all retire to the shade of the striped awning that forms the lean-to on the side of the School where the men eat and sleep. Fortunately Iain has his laptop with him as we are hoping that a little computer magic will aid our case.

We sense that they all sense something is up. People often ask us how we manage with so little Lao language, but really the body expresses all the emotions and words are only useful, then only sometimes, for filling in the detail.

We all squat on the dining table/multi-occupancy bed and Iain dings up the site that shows the miracle material we are intent on having in the roof lining; insulation. A long-time friend in Vientiane, fellow-Australian Marie Ryan, had told us about the material and we had looked up its website. I admit that the simple shots of rolls of fine bubble-wrap covered on both sides with a delicate but strong layer of aluminium foil are not a grabber. It doesn't help that the writing on the sales presentation is in Vietnamese. There is a strong though always understated feeling of resentment/ antagonism on the part of the Lao towards their Big Brother neighbour. Iain stresses that the rolls, though made in Vietnam, are imported from Thailand, the slightly less disliked of these two particular neighbours of the Lao whose political, geographical and social history is, well let's just say its complex.

The price of the wonder material is quoted on the site and I can see Mr. Khong has already worked out how many dollars this little piece of *falang* madness will cost. The underlying tension revolves around the fact that no other school in this area, or as far as Mr. Khong knows, any other area in the entire country, has an insulated roof. 'So what,' he says, though of course in Lao, 'if this wonder material really does reduce the heat in the insulated area by five or even ten degrees.' The unspoken addendum is a query as to why a school in the remote mountains built for people who are not known for their hospitality should be equipped with modern technology that is not available for the majority Lao Loum schools.

'It is only a rural school,' Mr. Khong protests through Chanthy and its impossible not to notice that Chanthy is inclined to agree. I know that Chanthy's own ego has taken a bit of a bashing from the most senior lads attending the present school because they chatter, obviously about him, behind his back, in their own language which they know full well he does not understand. I have seen his features get a little dark about this. But though I understand better than he could imagine what it is like to be an outsider in this type of situation, we're all in this together and we, that is Iain and I, are determined that a School for Phoujong is going to have an insulated roof; even if it is a first. Who knows it might be a trendsetter for the future.

Mr. Khong tries another tack mentioning that the roofing tin will be delivered very soon and he doesn't want any further delay to its installation. Then, as always, there is reference to the weather, the dreaded monsoon rains and that any delay to hammering on the roofing could well be a make or break decision.

Again, as always, it is gentle Thongkhanh who smoothes over the tensions by suggesting that we, that again is Iain and I, see how quickly we can get a hold of the rolls of insulation material and that meantime Builder Khong finds out what the time frame is for delivery of the roofing tin and that we talk over all this some more when we have a clearer idea of these timings and how they might, or might not, work. It's a calming masterstroke.

Down. Up. Down. Up. We hang on to the ever-moving roller coaster ride of emotions. But the day is not over yet.

Mr. Dith has been hanging around the periphery of all these happenings. Most commonly if he drives us up the mountain he simply drops us off at the building site, we pay him for the service, then he leaves us to our own devices and in the late afternoon we find someone else to give us a lift back down.

Until today he has been politely indifferent to the School at Phoujong. In common with the majority of NaLiners he gives the impression of viewing Phoujongers as a nuisance. Perhaps in rather the same way the majority of white Australians regard Australian Aborigines. So maybe it was the interest we had shown in his daughter's future or even because of our over-the-top display of happiness when the skeletal School at Phoujong first came into view that snagged at his heart. He sat with the other men as they looked at the computer pix of the insulation material and he listened to arguments for and against its use.

He stayed to the share the midday meal with us in the temporary shelter and in the following brief rest-time he joined in the conversation that Iain had with Chanthy who had asked him about his hearing aids. More *falang* magic.

But Mr. Dith still didn't leave and several times in

Under the shelter tarpaulin, Iain shows Chanthy and Mr. Dith his miniature hearing aids.

the afternoon, while Iain and I were busy take shots or going through Thongkhanh's account book, I saw him looking over the building and asking questions of the work-crew.

The light was already starting to soften and the intensity of the day's heat to lessen when he came alongside me to suggest that he could give us a lift back down the track. I explained that we needed to go on further than where he would normally turn off onto the Road to NaLin, but to go all the way into Muang Nan, an additional fifteen kilometres, thirty if one takes into account his trip back home from Muang Nan to his home. But Mr. Dith waved aside our concern,

'He is visiting his Father in Muang Nan,' Chanthy explains. 'He lives on the edge of the town. He wants to take us.' I thank Mr. Dith and accept his offer.

Obligingly Chanthy again contorts his small frame into the cramped space behind the driver/passenger bench seat and we set off on yet another bumpy downhill ride. Chanthy chatters happily along as he always does from his uncomfortable back perch position. He speaks in Lao, to Mr. Dith and it occurs to me that the Headman wants Chanthy tucked in with us so that he has someone with whom to converse on the trip. But quite abruptly Mr. Dith cuts in on Chanthy's chatter to ask something. Chanthy translates.

'Mr. Dith asks why do you want to build a School for Phoujong?'

It is something of a gob-smacker question, if for no other reason than no one else has thought to ask us. But as I turn my head to look at Mr. Ditch he smiles. In repose his features are somewhat stern but when he smiles this impression is totally superseded by one of warmth and interest. Still I can't help feeling it's a somewhat loaded question. I turn my head the other way to look for guidance from Iain.

'Because it needs one.' Iain responds.

'But why Phoujong specially?' comes the translated follow-up question.

My hackles rise, sensing the underlying prejudice. It seems even hotter in the cabin of the truck. The atmosphere is somewhat uncomfortable. 'Mr. Dith,' I say and carry on rather pompously, 'we understand something of the feelings you have about the villagers of Phoujong; the differences between you and them and even that perhaps you feel they are not grateful or even respectful. But we are not building a School for the villagers, for the men and women; we are building it for the children. You have two children. You know how vital education is...' I have to remember to stop and give Chanthy time to translate, 'these are kids with even less opportunity than yours. We'd like to have enough money to build schools for everyone. But we don't. So we hope to help those at the very bottom of the pile.' I use my hands to indicate what I mean. 'If it just helps improve the life of one child. If just one student goes on to become a teacher...or a nurse,' I add in a somewhat underhand blow!

'Its very good.' Mr. Dith replies and nods his head. 'Very good. A School for Phoujong. I like.'

9
ACCEPTANCE

At three in the morning Chanthy's mobile rings. He always respectfully keeps his phone inside his bedclothes in an attempt to stifle its ringtone but I am such a light sleeper that I wake with a start, knowing it must be bad news. It is. His mother is calling to tell him that her brother has died.

Death is never unexpected and never far away in Laos. It is as interwoven in life as is birth. This is something of what gives life its special bitter/sweet poignancy and refreshing lack of bullshit. Buachanh had only a few days previously taken a ten-hour ride on a local bus to visit this brother who lived in the far northeast of the country near the border with China. Before she left there had been no talk of illness or imminent death but maybe that was just another example of the Lao way.

Buachanh tells her son that his uncle has died within the last half hour from a heart attack. She plans to stay on in his home village to help with the funeral. There are no tears, just soft conversing in mutual support.

He hangs up and the three of us drift back into a light sleep.

The previous evening from our room in the Muang Nan hostel Iain had rung Marie Ryan in Vientiane and told her that the race to get the insulation was now on in earnest.

Marie Ryan

I don't think Marie would take exception to being described as something of a character. We had met her several years earlier when we were both working as volunteer Editors on an eighteen-month stint at the Voice VietNam Radio network. At that time Marie was struggling financially to survive by running the only English language bookshop in town. She has since written a book about the weird and wonderful experiences she had during this time. Its called *Cement Factory Number Nine*, which is the name she registered the business as, knowing that listing it as an English language bookshop would bring about a definite knockback by officialdom. It is an extremely amusing and prescient inside view of working within the strictures of a Communist government and well worth a read by anyone planning on visiting the country or even if you are not. It is available in electronic or hardcopy format and has been taken up in audio form by Singapore Airlines for passengers on their Asia routes.

With such experiences, plus many more, under her life-belt, Marie who is a highly qualified epidemiologist presently employed by the World Health Organisation and other big-time NGOs, we know she is certainly up to speed for the challenge of getting the insulation which was, incidentally, her idea in the first place and to also getting it up to us before Mr. Khong can get the roofing iron delivered.

Before eight that morning, by which time there have been several more muted mobile conversations between Chanthy and his Mother, his Father and as well his brother Jai and sister Bounlee, about the death in the family, Marie had emailed to tell us that she has already visited the factory office of the company that imports the rolls of insulation. She has paid for three and is right now arranging for them to be transported that very day by King of Bus from Vientiane to us, six hundred plus kilometres north, where we hope to be, in Luang Prabang. They are expected to be off-loaded at the bus station in town at around 5pm. Now all we have to do is get ourselves back up to LPB to be there in time to receive them

A few more emails and phone-chats confirm that she has managed to get them loaded on the bus.

'Let me know when it arrives,' Marie says, 'and whether it works. I am looking at putting it up into the ceiling space at my place.' Whether it works! Heavens! It better! After the sales job we have done on Mr. Khong and his merry men, plus the cost of US$350 of our supporters hard-won monies.

Marie's insulation being loaded into the luggage locker of the 'King of Bus'

We are all rather subdued on that morning's bus journey back up to LPB, all of us especially mindful of the poignancy of the roadside Prayer Houses.

There is a depth to the unusually quiet stillness surrounding Chanthy that I had begun to pick up on even before the news of his Uncle's death but that I had not given myself time to be anxious about.

159

Something else is worrying him but now was not the right time or place, to go there. How often in life we brush aside these inconvenient signs and later on have regrets.

Back in Luang Prabang we go our separate ways, Chanthy to his room and his college demands, us to our room and our emails and downloading. But by nine o'clock that night having kept in touch with Chanthy, who had been in constant mobile contact with the driver of the King of Bus, we know that our insulation will not arrive until after midnight. There have been unforeseen, but far from unusual, circumstances that have delayed its time of arrival several times. Chanthy gallantly offers to go back to the bus station on the outskirts of town just as soon as the driver warns him by mobile of his imminent arrival and we, less than gallantly, accept and fall into bed.

In his wake-up call to us at 6am Chanthy tells us that the rolls of insulation had finally arrived at half past midnight and that not wanting to risk leaving them in the bus station overnight he had hired a tuk-tuk to drive with them back to his room, where the driver and he had somehow manhandled them into the small space. He was already back at the bus station, with the insulation rolls, had bought tickets on that morning's bus down to Muang Nan that would be leaving in just over an hour and was

160

beginning negotiations with the bus company over a good price for transporting the bulky material. What a chap! Who wouldn't want to employ him.

On the return trip Chanthy regales us with the details of the wait for and arrival of the insulation which in the cooler temperatures of the early morning is beginning to look somewhat like a *Falang* Madness, though there is still a discernible and worrying lack of his usual vibrancy.

Back again in Muang Nan Mr. Dith is already waiting for us and our much vaunted magic cloth. He tells us that he had stayed with his parents overnight and as he ties the monster rolls onto the tray of his truck he happily assures us that the roofing tin will not be delivered to the Phoujong site until mid-afternoon. He appears more than somewhat pleased for us to have to have pipped Mr. Khong at the post. We chow down our habitual *pho* at the bus-station café with the Noi family but on the way out of the settlement Mr. Dith pulls over to one side of the road saying that he would like to make a quick call on his Father, and invites us to come in. Naturally we agree, having been told that his Father is ill, but unaware of just how ill.

In fact his Dad is dying. He is dying a degrading death. Some weeks ago he had been diagnosed with stomach cancer and was offered the 'opportunity' of an operation at the hospital in Sayaboury. During the operation it would seem that the cancerous tumour had been excised, though its unclear if all of it has been removed and so whether or not the operation could be considered, in medical terms at least, successful. A stoma has been inserted into what remains of his bowel. But after telling the family there is nothing more they can do and that the hospital had no collection bags for excreta Mr. Dith senior has been sent home with a small number of much used terry toweling nappies. The tiny amount of food and fluid he manages to take in is excreted more or less immediately into these nappies. If there is a smell its not of human waste or even fear but perhaps of resignation and acceptance. His skeletal figure lies half propped up on mattresses and cushions.

Headman Dith squats down on his haunches beside his Father and holds his hand, stroking the thin skin while his Mother welcomes us with a graciousness that her innate dignity enables her to hold on to, even in such circumstances.

The elderly man nods towards us and through his son and then Chanthy, he conveys that he wishes to return to the hospital and for the doctors there to 'put his stomach and things back inside.'

Hung on the wall above him is a tinted photograph of a young man, full of vigour, in the uniform of the Pathet Lao. His middle-aged children move about the single room, conversing with their Mother in low voices, bringing what small comforts they can.

Back in the truck, even Chanthy's naturally ebullient spirit flounders and there is a silence while we all, individually, absorb what we have just experienced. It would be insulting to vocalise reassuring tut-tuts.

Then a few kilometres outside the settlement we drive unexpectedly into a strong-smelling smoky burn-off. It is so dense that for a second or two it obscures the track. As we regain the view Iain asks in a surprised tone, 'What is all that about?'

'Chinese', Headman Dith informs, with little warmth in his voice.

From both sides of the road the land, which until yesterday had been screened by a row of trees has been laid bare. Not a casual tidy-through ready for the season's replanting of hops, rice or assorted veggies, but a slash-back to the raw, red newly-churned earth. No trees or bushes left standing. Several bright yellow front-end loaders and tractors are charging about fiercely completing the job.

In the distance, now revealed by the disappearance of the vegetation but shrouded in the

Hundreds of hectares of land being cleared by Chinese entrepreneurs to grow bananas

blue haze from the burn-off, there is a collection of single-storey simple but substantial buildings. They do not look like they would welcome visitors.

Mr. Dith was, in common with Thongkhanh, also born in 1967, the year in which US General Curtis LeMay pronounced that the answer to ending the Vietnam War, known here as the American War, and its deadly 'sideshows' in Laos and Cambodia, was to 'bomb them back to the Stone-Age.'

He's seen them come and he's seen them go. The French, the Americans and their Allies including Australians; now it's the turn of the Chinese. We feel for him that it's a relief after the visit to his Father, to pick up and explain the details. It's a replacement space to park his distress.

The essence of the deal is that the Chinese, there is always a slight edge to his tone, have signed a ten year contract with the twenty village families of Ban Phon, one of the dozen or so villages along the valley of the

Haidsaik River, for a lease over 400 hectares of their land. They plan to set up banana plantations. The fruit will be exported by truck to China. The border at the burgeoning Special Economic Zone of Botem, is 300 kilometers away. For a wage the villagers will do the hands-on work at the plantations while the management will be Chinese.

It was entrepreneurs from Laos's massive northern neighbour who made the first approach. There were village meetings at which, after an initial agreement to proceed had been agreed upon, the gritty details were worked out. First up permissions were sought from and given by the Lao central government. These are 'fraternal' societies. Tiny poor minnow Communist Laos and huge wealthy tuna Communist China. They already have complex deep economic ties, most especially concerning the waters of the Mekong and mineral mining.

I ask if there was 'a vote'. This required further explanation. A sealed box with slips of paper? Or a public show of hands? And did everyone get to have a voice? Land owners only? Men only?

'Everyone just agreed.'

A very Lao way of resolution.

And the figure?

Five million kip per year for each hectare. So one billion kip a year all up. Which works out to each family getting roughly US$1,500 annually. US$130 a month. $US4 a day. The zinger appeal in the contract surely is that the monies are paid two years in advance.

As anyone who has spent time in China knows, they don't mess about. This deal will inevitably bring about much-needed rural infrastructure improvements in the form of roads and bridges. Hopefully, though funded by Chinese wanting fast, safe transport routes, these will be built by the Lao and so will increase work skills as well as putting money in Lao pockets; slowly enabling the movement from a 19th century colonial barter economy to a 21st century cash economy.

There will of course inevitably be accompanying downsides.

When asked if our friends, the villagers of NaLin, have also been approached by Chinese agri-business operators with similar plans, Mr. Dith nods and tell us; 'But we all said No. We don't want to be owned by the Chinese.'

The obvious question is, 'So why did the villagers from Ban Phon sign up?

His reply is immediate and unusually judgmental for a Buddhist Lao.

'Because they are lazy and want money for

nothing.'

There follows quite a long silence.

When Mr. Dith speaks again it is to say: 'In Luang Namtha, the Lao Province further north, that borders China, the Chinese did the same. But when they didn't like the flavour, or perhaps it was only the size or shape, of the bananas that were produced, they just walked away. Leaving the villagers to get rid of the banana plants and to replant their own crops. No compensation.'

And after another long silence: 'I am thinking of standing down as Headman. So is Thongkhanh. Five years in the job is long enough. There is too much stress. It's time to hand over to the next generation. They want different things.'

Including a School for Phoujong I think, but do not say. We, Iain and I, and all the people who have made such generous individual donations to the Project, we are all part of this change. We had no idea when we first visited NaLin that the Valley, the Village, the Villagers were on the cusp of great change. How could we have known?

I recall the words of a longtime friend at home in Australia who assured me that building The Road, The Culverts and now The School would bring change. 'Well I certainly hope so, ' I had responded somewhat waspishly. But of course we were referring to two different sorts of change. There would be bad as well as good changes.   This is the age-old conundrum and we had to believe that the people we had come to know in the Valley and to whom we were now so attached would embrace the changes and use them to their positive advantage.

Better roads, schools and even hospitals might mean that no one would die in the manner of Mr. Dith senior.

I glance at the tired face of this man who is younger than my own children. He is going through what in our home society would be blandly dismissed as a mid-life crisis. Father dying, daughter finishing school and wanting to experience life, and he himself confronted everywhere by change, change, change.

***

Our arrival in Phoujong is announced by the sounds of our truck as it groans and clatters across the culvert and crashes gears chugging up the hillside to reach the building site. Mr. Khong, trying too hard to look relaxed, is surrounded by a mob of children. The bush telegraph has let them know that we are bringing white-fella magic and despite it being Saturday and a school-free day they have come to bear witness.

We hop out of the cabin, trying not to look triumphalist.

The insulation rolls are untied from the back and carried like sacrifices into the framework body of The School. Thank heavens for the children whose chatter fills the somewhat awkwardness.

Mr. Khong stands back as his left-hand man, Mr. Zoy, tears open the heavy-duty clear plastic protective cover. Thongkhanh, as always a calming as well as cheerful presence assists him to begin to unroll the aluminium coated plastic bubble material. The children press forward while the workers remain carefully impassive.

Thongkhanh, ever ready, proffers big scissors, as between him and Zoy they roll out a long piece and snip it through. It becomes apparent that the measurement had been decided upon in advance of our arrival. I notice now that a rough homemade ladder is already in place and secured to one of the support pylons. Zoy scrambles up the ladder holding on to one end of the cut strip while Thongkhanh feeds it up to him. Its bright metal flashes in the sunlight. The children express delight and I hold my breath. It is of course immensely hot.

Barefoot Zoy clambers dexterously along the roof beams and hammers one end of the material into the ridgeline letting the body of it flow down to the far

Thongkhanh and Zoy on rafters with insulation

end. There are c a l l e d instructions given from below by Mr. Khong. It is decided that for maximum effect the material needs to be turned over. Between them Zoy and Thonghkhanh manage this cumbersome process.

It is no exaggeration to say that in the shade even this first small piece has created the drop in felt heat is immediate.

Zoy and Thongkhanh repeat the process, this time letting the material down from the ridgeline to the front of the building. This time they get it turned correct way up first off. By the time everyone stops for the meal break in the middle of the day, half the building has been sun-screened and the beneficial impact the process has been made is clear to everyone.

While the children play now-you-feel-it-now-you-don't games inside the skeletal building with the sunlight and shadow, oohing and aahing over the obvious difference made by this delicate material we squat down with the work-crew under the tarpaulin and join in the meal. Thongkhanh has barbecued tiny fish for Iain and I and serves up buffalo laap for the men. There are of course inexhaustible supplies of sticky rice.

In a sure sign that this a special occasion, there is Beer Lao. Mr. Khong, in a spirit of generous acceptance raises his bottle toward Iain. There is a huge feeling of comradeship.

I cannot be sure of course but I do so hope that these words have managed to capture the emotions of that day's experiences, because, though there were many more to come, this day encapsulates for me what building a School for Phoujong has been all about.

10 THUNDERBOLT

Exhaustion wasn't the word for it. We, perhaps particularly me because of my additional struggle with painful knees, were beyond exhaustion. Mental challenges are always at least if not more exhausting than mere physical calls on strength and during the last few days we had certainly found it necessary to summon up every wee dram of our mental strength. So we decided that if we were to complete the Project without falling over we needed to be kinder to ourselves. Having both of us been born going at 100% speed in top gear one of our hardest lessons to learn with age is to pace ourselves.

After the success with the insulation we had stayed one more day paying trade suppliers bills in Muang Nan and visiting 'family' in NaLin where we further admired the Sisombuth's new ablutions area, played with baby Jarrah, watched Binh distil her newest batch of Lao-lao and assisted carpenter Sengchan's wife, Ms. Lar, sort through her hop harvest, discarding the empty, weightless, colourless and therefore useless seed sacs, keeping only the weighty, dark-brown full ones. It was a relaxing, domestically pleasing time.

Ms. Lar with her hops seeds

It seems that everyone in NaLin knew about the extravagant reception that had been given to the roofing insulation. There were even hilarious stories that one of the workers on the School site was planning on making 'cooling jackets' from the fabric with plans to create his fortune by selling these in Luang Prabang's Night Market!

Before leaving we call on neighbour, Ms. On, who is already two weeks past the due date for the arrival of her second baby. In Australia anxiety surrounding births has somewhat faded into the background, except of course for the mother-to-be. But in Laos where the infant mortality rates, though decreasing, still stand at just under 6% of all live births and where they are highest of all in isolated areas such as NaLin and Phoujong, everyone is aware of the very real dangers to both mother and child, of birthing. We leave her with our good wishes, which were no doubt rather poor compensation for the lack of medical care.

It is with a great sense of relief that we arrive back in Luang Prabang. The elegant town was established in a beautiful setting at the confluence of the Mekong and Nam Khan rivers and even in the face of many onslaughts it has managed to hold on to much of its appeal and charm.

A great deal of this is due to the atmosphere of calm created by the more than thirty *wats* elaborately decorated with gold paint that range in age from brand new to five hundred years and that are everywhere, including unexpected nooks and crannies, across the heart of town. The 3,000 novices and monks, whose orange robes glow in the streets, as their wearers glide to prayers and to class, are its defining expression.

Even a total non-follower of any religious structure such as myself cannot fail but find solace in the seemingly constant hum of prayer chanting and

At Wat Xieng Thong, Luang Prabang's oldest temple

the regular day and night rituals of drum beating.

We often talk about how different the town would feel if instead of 3,000 followers of the Buddha there were an identical number of same-aged lads in individualistic clothing; baseball caps, sleeveless sloganed, tee-shirts and purposely torn jeans, just aimlessly roaming the streets at all hours.

When we hugged our adieus outside Chanthy's room we suggest that he too might enjoy a small break from the full-on demands we had all been under. We were very conscious that his were even greater because although he had arranged with his boss to take un-paid time off from work, on the understanding that his job may or may not be still available when he wants to come back to it, such was his confidence in his job-skills, he is still attempting to keep up with his college class-work. There is something unusual in the way he mentions he'd prefer not to make a time for tomorrow's get together, because he had phone calls to make. So we leave him after arranging only that we would be in touch.

Funeral rituals along one of Luang Prabang's main streets

We have our own list of places we especially enjoy eating in LPB and we both knew what particular meal appealed to each of us right then: the comfort of western food. We linger, which is something unusual for us, over the meal. Even more unusual, before going to bed we don't even get the diary up to date, download shots and footage or file the receipts.

In the morning we take a leisurely cycle alongside the Mekong, stopping to photograph two elaborate funeral rituals as well as preparations for a wedding, before having another restorative western meal, breakfast of muesli and fresh coffee.

By the time we arrive back at the Mekong Charm the day is already heating up but I reckon I can squeeze in half an hour of knitting on the balcony before the sweat in my palms puts an end to it. Knitting is my great relaxer. I am knitting a really boring fine gauge blue-black totally plain, shawl-collared sweater for our son. It calls upon no imagination or talent, which is just as well because both are in short supply.

As I knit I watch a young lad of about six or seven: life's magic age. He is the grandson of the man next door, Thongdy, whom we had first met as a boatman on the Mekong but who had a stroke a couple of years back and who is still struggling to walk efficiently. He has told us stories about his work with the American Secret Service during the American War and has even shown us photographs and a diary he kept at that time. No longer able to operate the family owned ferryboat because he has lost the use of his right arm as well as the right side of his body, we have admired the tenacity with which he pushes himself to re-establish his strength.

His grandson has obviously inherited Thongdy's capacity for internal imagination and determination because almost every day he sets up his solo game of thong throwing. First of all he paces out the distance. I can see him counting under his breath. He places a forlornly worn solo thong, which he has quite apparently collected from the garbage, at one end of this roadside 'court' and another at the opposite end. He then 'hides' behind the concrete electricity pole that sprouts from the broken concrete of the pavement midway between both ends and with deft movements, accompanied by guttural sounds, he 'attacks' first one thong, then the other by throwing small pieces of discarded timber or even concrete.

He knows I am watching him. We eyeballed each other when Iain and I first moved in and to begin with he sulked about my presence. But then, as I gave small appreciate cheers and even gentle claps over his successes, though I had no idea really whether they were successes or failures as I couldn't work out the rules of his game, he started to include me in his performance. Sometimes there was a small salute or even a perfunctory wave. Today he even looks up to make sure I am watching before he starts his routine. The world is wonderful when you are seven. Perhaps it is never as wonder-filled again.

I am just starting to feel the heat getting to me when Iain comes out onto the balcony. I can feel the cool rush of air-conditioned air gush from the door behind him. He has been doing downloads and has that odd look about him that he always gets when doing this job; other-worldly, dazed, slightly boss-eyed.

'Chanthy has just rung to say he is on his way over,' he announces and disappears back inside. I decide to stay and finish my row, actually my round, as I am knitting on a circular needle. So I am still there when only a few minutes later Chanthy draws up on a motorbike belonging to one of his myriad cousins and parks it near where my young playmate is gaming. I hadn't expected Chanthy to turn up so quickly; he usually gives us half an hour's warning. But I don't have time to wonder about this before I realise, even more unexpectedly, that Chanthy is in a confused state. I quickly gather up my handiwork but before I can go inside Chanthy is already crossing the river front street and I notice his frowning agitation as he runs his fingers through his strong black hair. He has not seen me on my first floor balcony and I quickly go inside and announce to Iain, 'I saw Chanthy. There's something wrong with him.' Before Iain can mentally compute any of this Chanthy knocks on our door, Iain is opening it and Chanthy is bursting into the room, looking as though he is about to explode into tears.

'I have problem, ' he announces in a breathless strangled voice without even saying good-morning. 'Oh Chanthy,' we say simultaneously, both moving towards him, 'what's the matter? What has happened?' But Chanthy won't let us hug him. Instead he covers his face with his hands and his whole body begins to shake. 'Sit down. Sit down, Chanthy'. Iain drags the heavy stool he has been using as an office chair across to him. Chanthy doesn't see this and instead sits, or rather crouches on the edge of the bed with his face in his hands. We perch ourselves each side of him, stroking his arms and making soothing noises. 'Try to tell us Chanthy, ' Iain says, 'that way we can help you.'

So out it tumbles, his story of joy and grief.

Of course its woman troubles. But though that's a relief to us, its no such thing for Chanthy. His first real love affair. His broken heart. His inexperience with the ways of the world. Pretty small beer you could be, almost, forgiven for brushing aside such dramatics. But is there anything, anything at all, so devastating in its ability to unhinge you as the savage intensity of irrational affairs of the heart?

If you need someone to give sensible advice over such matters it would be best not to approach us. Our so-far fifty-plus-year relationship was created from a havoc of madness, torn from a maelstrom of lunacy. So how can we but cry with him, sympathize and reach out to find a way to deal with his pain.

Others, more moderate with their feelings would, more than likely most wisely, suggest he should pull up his socks, get on with his life or spout other truisms such as: 'there are plenty more fish in river of life,' which of course would be accurate, but would only heap on the distress and also be certain to be rejected.

Iain opens a Coca-Cola from the small bar-fridge in the room and between gulps of the hideously sweet, but very cold, liquid Chanthy manages to come down off his initial outburst and regain his English language abilities, enabling us to gradually piece together what has happened.

It would seem that his sweetheart, who is a few years younger than Chanthy and comes from a small village northeast of Luang Prabang was visiting the family of a girlfriend in town when she met Chanthy. There seems to have been no restraint on either side. The joy lasted for only under two weeks before she had to leave, accompanied by the girlfriend, to return to VietNam where she is studying on a much-sought-after scholarship awarded by the host government. She is now in the second year of a five-year degree course.

The agony of this separation was much increased by her revelation that she has a boyfriend, not very long-term but long-term enough to be certain to cause problems, in the city where she is studying. This about-to-be-ousted boyfriend is a fellow-Lao.

Since their separation she and Chanthy have been in frequent contact by mobile; which at least explained the amount of time Chanthy spent on his phone as well as his agitation that I had picked up on. She had told him that when she went back to VietNam she had attempted to end the relationship with the other student but his reaction had been to become aggressive to the point of stalking her both on her phone and in person. It was a very twenty-first century scenario.

'What do you want to happen?' Iain asks in a calming tone.

'I want to be with her,' Chanthy responds without hesitation. "I want to look after her and to make this other man understand that she wants me, not him.'

'And what does she say she wants?' I venture to ask.

'That is what she wants too,' he says.

I had to ask. 'Are you sure? She isn't just playing games with your heart?'

'No. No.' Chanthy says with strength.

Having just started a new term at university meant that the student girlfriend would not be coming back to Laos for at least three months. Three unbearable months as far as Chanthy was concerned and by his account, for her too.

For a Lao, winning an educational scholarship is

BIG. It's the stuff of dreams. It's the gigantic leap out of poverty that all parents want for their children and that all those children also want both for their parents and for themselves. It is impossible to overestimate its lifetime positive effect on the student and her entire family. It is not something that any student could ever, ever, turn their back on, for whatever reason and most certainly not for an affair of the heart. That is just not the way life operates in Laos.

So with that as a given it would seem that the only possible way out of this conundrum is for Chanthy to visit VietNam and there to make it totally clear to the other suitor that he is yesterday's man and to move on.

With a now much calmer Chanthy we discuss possibilities, state of play, game plan and actions. At some stage over the next few hours, spent in our room, in an air-conditioned café and later at the bus-station, where we are now so well known that staff there greet us by our first names, decisions begin to be made.

There are a multitude of mobile calls to his sweetheart as well as to his Mother in NaLin and Father on the worksite at Phoujong, from where, almost incidentally, Thongkhanh tells us that the entire roof is now covered in insulation. Roof? Insulation? Oh yes, that other life. Such is the impact of this thunderbolt on all our emotional states that these events appear to be happening in a far-way and foreign place.

Between us all it is finally decided that Chanthy will take that evening's thirty-hour, overnight bus journey up and over the high mountains into VietNam and on to the large city where his sweetheart is attending college. In a flurry of activity Iain travels around town riding pillion on the tolerant cousin's motorbike. Maps, Vietnamese monies and cross-border visa photographs are obtained along with an international simcard for his mobile. 'I will keep in touch,' Chanthy promises.

In a small space of clear thinking I do manage to ask Chanthy what his parents think about all these decisions and tell him that we definitely do not, I stress the do not, want his parents to think that we are persuading him one way or the other in his choices. As a parent myself I know I would feel extremely ticked off if I thought that my child was being unwillingly persuaded by other adults, especially, lets face it, *falang* adults.

Chanthy is adamant that they are very much aware that these are his own decisions and adds that his Mother and Father want him to tell us they are happy we can help make his journey happen. But I have been a parent for long enough to know both

Thongkhanh and Buachanh must be torn with misery and querying their own decision to let their son, this child who has broken free from the usual restraints, to move to the city and make a life separate from the rules of family behaviour. I know if I was in their place that is how I would feel.

Nobody but nobody can serve it up to you like your own children.

It is now we are grateful that a couple of years back we had encouraged Chanthy to get his first-ever passport. He had in fact used it earlier this year when his doolally boss decided on the spur of the moment to make a quick trip into Thailand to get the lowdown on any tourist traps he could emulate and to take English-speaking Chanthy with him. That visit had been an eye-opener for Chanthy and the basis for many of the amusing stories with which we had seen him regale his family as well as people in his village and in Phoujong.

But this will be solo foreign travel and we knew that this visit was going to be an eye-opener too though on a quite different level of experience. As we wave him onto the big sleeper bus that evening, loaded down with pre-cooked food to see him through the night, plus bottles of water and his small travel bag he looks so small, so vulnerable, so naïve.

Iain had earlier given him a man-to-man talk

about keeping an eye out for any 'characters' on the bus and to be careful not get ripped off by tourist touts as well as customs and immigration people on both sides of the border. Having loaned him the cotton passport and money hold-all he wears permanently around his neck when we are on the road, Iain now instructs him to 'Wear it concealed under your shirt and never take it off.'

It has been arranged that his girlfriend will meet him from the bus. The plan is for him to stay only three days but during that time they will resolve where they want their relationship to go. In a candid addendum I found somewhat revelatory Iain tells him: 'Let the other bloke know you are now her boyfriend. Don't get into a fight of any sort with him. Be firm. But not too fair.'

Loaded down with all this anxious advice Chanthy sallies forth while, without any further words being exchanged, we go to our room and our bed, rendered speechless by the day's dramas.

186

11 ANTI-RAIN DANCE

'No more rain, Hughie, please, no more rain,' we silently beg the sky-god.

I stand on the rough broken pavement outside the Saylomgnen Guesthouse peering disconsolately through the downpour trying, as when I was a child, to find enough blue sky to make a sailor a pair of trousers. That's what is required now: a child's resolute belief.

Despite the anxiety over the rain, my word, it feels so good to be back in Muang Nan. Even Luang Prabang has begun to appear confrontingly crowded and busy. I am aware of my small village upbringing creeping in around the edges of my thought patterns. I wonder to what places of the heart aging Chinese will return in say fifty years time when all their childhood memories will be of 'small' towns of ten million people.

In the week we have been away, 'in town' so much has happened. On my determined mission to keep all our supporters in the loop I have been busy sending the following email. It is impossible to estimate how it will resonate with them when they read it under such different circumstances than it was written.

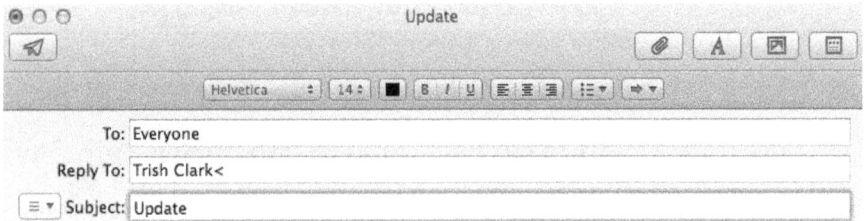

● ○ ⊖	Update				

To: Everyone

Reply To: Trish Clark<

Subject: Update

Sabaidee everyone...

An update about a School for Phoujong.

In your very welcome responses many of you have inquired, 'what about the loo?' As well you may, after enduring all the months of pooh-talk! The good news is the loo is going well too. The septic tank has been dug and lined with concrete blocks so its 'just' the above ground walls, roof and plumbing plus pie-dishes left to do.

Equally good is that today Iain and Chanthy withdrew 55 million from the bank.

They made payments of 48,128,000

Which should have left them with cash in hand of

6,880,000.

When the cash was counted there was 6,840,000.

A discrepancy of 40,000.

or in translation FIVE DOLLARS!!!!!!!!!! short! and I shall dock this amount from Iain's pocket money this week.

Its fun playing with these huge figures and just as huge piles of banknotes!

The atmosphere on the work-site is still abuzz with quiet confidence and mutual trust.

It has been a BIG week in the Valley of the Hadsaik River.

Ms.On was finally taken up to the hospital in Luang Prabang where she gave birth, over two weeks past her due date, to a healthy baby boy. Mother and son are doing well. They are both now back in NaLin, Ms.On, sitting on a raised platform by a fire (in this heat!) looking tired, but happy. First-time mothers are not allowed visitors for a month. But for number two and all-subsequent births, visitors are welcomed by invitation as soon as the mother and baby are home. All mothers eat 'hot'...heat-inducing foods...and are given a daily rubdown with warmed water. Ms. On now has two sons. This new boy will not be given a name for a month. This is to trick the phi into not knowing he has arrived. Or he will be given a tender nickname and then his lifelong name when he is around a month old, when the phi are considered to have given up the ghost (oops ...lame joke) and moved on.

We were invited to visit On and her Mother, who left the noisy extended family mob eating and playing cards in an adjoining part of the house, to join us and in a woman-to-woman chat I made sure to let them know that it is the MAN whose part in procreation determines the sex of the baby. Not the woman. Or even what you eat! Though I am now at the crossroads of wondering myself if all these 'facts' that we are so sure about are 100% accurate! We all laughed. And they asked how these childbirth habits and ideas differed from those in Australia. Yes... well...

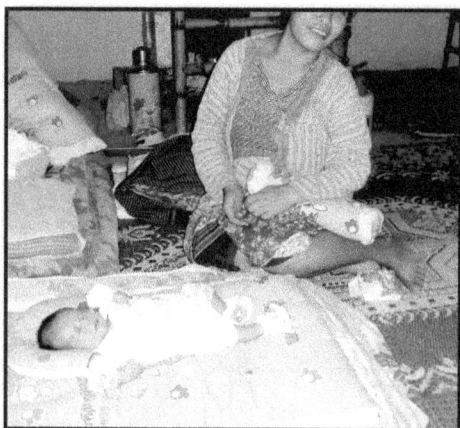

Ms. On and her baby

Sadly, at the other end of the life cycle, Mr. Thondy Thongsamou's wife died, suddenly, of a heart attack in the middle of the night.

Thondy has become a special friend of ours,

based originally on the fact that he is a couple of years even older than Iain! And they like to josh one another about this amazing fact! Thongdy is the village morphon, or spirit man, and was a Buddhist monk for thirty-three years. An auspicious number here because only the Buddha has 33 teeth. Thongdy's wife, with whom he has three children was only in her sixties.

Because she was suffering with severe chest pains the villagers had taken her to the clinic fifteen kilometres or so down the track at Khoktum, where she died.

This is an almost bigger sorrow than her actual death.

No one wants to die outside of their own home.

Especially not with strangers.

The clinic doctor, an excellent chap whom we have met, sensibly allowed Thongdy and the villagers to carry her body back up the track, on the promise that she would not be taken back into the village, but laid to rest in the forest. I can only assume he insisted on this promise on the grounds of health.

Here, at the turn off onto The Road to NaLin she was given a simple funeral, her body cremated and this week her bones will be cleaned and placed in a funerary jar. This is where her phi *will remain too, rather than in the home she shared with Thongdy. And this is what is so hard for him to bear.*

Chanthy is home from a very brief visit to his sweetheart in the Vietnamese coastal city of Vinh, that involved two thirty-hour exhausting sleeper-bus rides and much life learning. She is a cross-border scholarship student from the north of Laos and from photographs very softly pretty, with an almost 1940s look. They sorted things out. And the irrepressible Chanthy returned with a fund of amusing stories about Vietnam, the Vietnamese and such eye-popping experiences as riding up fifteen floors!!! in an elevator and wow! most amazing of all...the sea...!!!!! the sound it makes, like breathing in and out, the vast empty horizon, the feeling of lurking danger! He assured us that he bravely put his head, briefly, beneath the water! that the water tastes salty and why should that be so? A question I found I could not immediately answer with any simplicity.

Then there was the food, not as good as in Laos, especially as there is no sticky rice!

The constant noise, especially of car and motorbike horns! all night!

The fact that no one spoke Lao! or English!

And worst of all, that there are no wats!

Churches, yes, but, well...

No wats!

Chanthy and his girlfriend have come to some agreement of which we have of course not inquired, we shall all take it a step at a time!

I am just glad I am a grandmother and have been through all this plus more, a fair number of times!

The wet season is all but upon us. Yesterday there was a huge deluge with thunder and lightening, please do an Anti-Rain Dance, as we have perhaps three at the most four more big truck deliveries of materials for the loo. The upside of this was the scenery from the bus on the way back down, fast-moving vast curtains of cloud wreathed the mountains, but, no more rain for a couple of weeks please Hughie.

***

We stay overnight in NaLin as we realise Chanthy will want to spend time with his Mother talking through decisions that were made during his visit to VietNam. Bouchanh is so fine-boned, so tiny but there is a steely strength about her. We exchange mother-to-mother smiles of understanding as we offer respectful *nops* to each other.

Thongkhanh is of course up at Phoujong in his Building Site Supervisor capacity. But Bounlee is here

193

with baby Jarrah and we talk through an idea that has been bubbling away in my febrile brain having surfaced very shortly before we left Australia.

Neville Jennings and his wife Leonie, who have made a sizeable donation to the Project and who are both retired from long careers in the field of education, came up with the suggestion of Sistering the School at Phoujong with the Primary School at Chillingham, where Neville now volunteers as the Ethics Teacher.

The small village of Chillingham is set deep into the caldera of Mt.Wollumbin/Warning in the lip-smackingly beautiful New South Wales north coast area of the upper Tweed Valley. Like Phoujong, it has a small river and is surrounded by rainforest. That is about where any similarity between the villages ends.

The students Neville teaches come from your regular Australian families so, although they are almost certainly unaware of the fact, they are among the most privileged and fortunate children anywhere in the world. Apart from its very appealing country-style architecture, their small school, with a total of thirty-five students, is brim-full with an enormous range of brain and body stimulating equipment, highly trained, promptly paid teachers and, yes, good loos.

Official Sistering is something I had contemplated

when we first started off on The Road to NaLin. I had looked into what was involved. It seemed to be a win/win scheme and I even went so far as to make introductory phone-calls and get the paperwork underway. But there I fell off my horse. It was just too much to organize on top of all that was required to initially establish us officially in Australia as a licensed charity and kick, and I mean *kick*-start the actual fund-raising for the Road.

But when the idea came out of the woodwork again, this time presented by someone happy and willing to do the legwork we pounced on Neville determined not to let him go.

Geeing people up with enthusiasm is a tough call but Neville was the man for the job; an interesting combination of ideas, flair and work-ethic, he sings in the Chillingham Voices, the local choir. During the most recent of the group's performances, a traditional jazz concert, Neville wore a black suit and snazzy trilby and was quite obviously channeling Leonard Cohen.

Neville (Leonard) Jennings

Neither of us had any idea how to run with the idea of Sistering or Partnering the schools but we thought that a good start would be to meet with the Principal, Vicki Roach and it was at this meeting that I watched Neville do what I have since seen him do many times in conversations, always successfully: let the chat flow, encourage people to speak, listen as if you are hanging off their every word and then, just as you feel the chat begin to ebb,

Chillingham Principal Vicki Roach

whammo, agree totally to the suggestion they didn't actually make but with enough force that they think they did. And you are home and hosed. Very subtle yet clever. I have no idea if Neville, whose voice is quietly contemplative, operates like this knowingly or if it is just a natural in-built talent.

By the end of that first meeting Ms. Roach was certain she had suggested it would be an excellent idea to introduce the children to each other through the medium of their drawings. Neville would ask students in his Ethics Class and we would ask students at Phoujong, as well as NaLin, partly because we were initially so unsure of what the response at

Phoujong would be, to draw pictures of themselves, their family members, their homes, their environment and anything else they wanted to share.

So here I am in NaLin explaining all this to Bounlee, who immediately picks up on the idea. To seal the deal I produce from my day-bag packets of crayons and plain paper, that I had optimistically purchased in LPB, because I knew her school had neither. She tells me she would require more of these and I tell her I will also suggest to Kaojien that his students become involved. But I can tell she thinks we have Buckley's.

In that she was incorrect. Kaojien gladly accepts the crayons and paper, also requests more and assures us his students will draw their lives to illustrate them to other children. As simple as that. We had anticipated the idea as being so totally foreign that we would have difficulty explaining why and how; but perhaps just because they belong to the international fraternity of teachers Bounlee and Kaojien know exactly what we are on about and what's more they immediately pick it up as a positive, fun idea.

We doss down on mats on the floor for the night, and despite, or perhaps because of the discomforts, I surface to full consciousness in the pre-dawn with the lightness of heart I have come to anticipate with pleasure whenever we stay over in Chanthy's family home.

During the night, woken by the sound of unwanted rain on the roof, I hear baby Jarrah's muffled demands for a feed of breast-milk and the muted voices of Chanthy and his Mother, no doubt talking over what had been decided during his visit to VietNam. They have a very close relationship, Chanthy and Buachanh. Village family life in Laos is the very glue that holds the positive aspects of the whole country's social structures in a steadiness.

***

A couple of years back when brother Jai had chosen a young woman whom he wanted to marry the suggested relationship was knocked on the head by Thongkhanh and Buachanh as being an unsuitable match. When Binh came into Jai's orbit she was found to be acceptable. Of course this guidance, some would call it interference, in such a personal matter as a life-partner would be seen as outrageous in our home society. But as with a great many other of life's perspectives, for me living in Laos is also challenging this up-to-now given. In the unavoidable day-to-day domestic closeness of Lao village life it would be impossible to dissemble and fudge one's character flaws, so happily Jai's wife Binh, mother of their son Sydney, has come up trumps.

The cockerels crow to each other. Children's voices, so universally the same, begin to break the surface. Adult footfalls take off in the direction of the rice paddy. Chickens and ducks start to scratch and peck in the dirt for tasty morsels. The fire has been lit out back by Buachanh; the daily ration of rice is being steamed. The day has begun.

Because it is a Saturday there is no hurried need to get pupils ready for school. We mooch around like people do on weekends at home. Friends, extended family and neighbours plus dogs and chooks drift in and out of each other's places. We take down our mosquito nets, roll up our mats and perform perfunctory slosh-over ablutions before squatting by the smoky fire to finger up some sticky rice.

But just because its Saturday doesn't mean it's a free day for the women. As I wander through the village many of them are busy sorting the results of the garlic harvest. It's a very communal happening. They sit in groups on small low handmade stools. Some of them sit on bright sarongs spread on the dirt. All of them are surrounded by evidence of their gardening skills. The smell is overpowering. They invite me to sit with them as they banter and laugh while they peel the outside soil-smudged greenery from the bodies of the plants and make them up into large bunches that will sell for 15,000kip or about a dollar, in the market at Muang Nan. No doubt they

199

are chatting about the important life matters women share in groups all around the world: their husbands, children and the latest gossip as well as money and sex though probably not much about politics. Laos is a bland politics-free zone. I have brought photographs of my children and grandchildren to show them because I know they are genuinely interested.

When newcomers to Australia are asked, 'what do you miss about your Homeland?' they invariably shrug their shoulders while trying to put their emotions into some coherence and just as invariably the best they can manage, wherever they come from is to say, 'The Life.' And this is it. The Life. This here and now, sitting on the

NaLin women bunching garlic

village pathway alongside people with whom you have shared experiences, peeling garlic buds.

We are waiting, in the loose sense of the word, for Mr. Dith to be ready to drive us up that track again to Phoujong. But by the time he is ready a couple of teenaged girls of the village, probably sisters, have set up a 'shop' in the shade of their timber family home and are busy running electricity leads out through the open shutters to a primitive blender. We watch as they set up a row of jars some filled with violent coloured powders others with equally hideously coloured worm-shaped pieces of, well who knows what really, but most likely gelatin. A tub of water is dragged up by their assumed brothers from the village water-stand and a handwritten sign which Chanthy tells us advertises Drinks For Sale is propped in front of a few empty cracked cups.

We are encouraged, prompted, nay instructed, to be their first customers. A jug is dipped into the water, spoonfuls of various powders of our choice are added and when

impromptu drinks stall in NaLin

this concoction has been blended a few of the 'worms' are added. Oh gosh its hard to look enthusiastic, harder still to swallow and almost impossible not to puke but instead to smack our lips with pleasure. We are encouraged to buy further cupfuls but we pike out and instead insist on buying cups all round.

This goes down very well but fortunately Mr. Dith who has been watching our discomfort with amusement announces the 'the daily bus to Phoujong has resumed service and is leaving immediately.'

We are so excited at the prospect of seeing what progress has been made during our week's absence that we feel we might throw up with anticipation, or is it the result of the ultra-sweet liquid now swirling in our stomachs?

We have hardly driven out of NaLin and on through the even tinier settlement of Houahye when we see numerous fires in the hillside. The black smoke from them plumes high into the blue sky. Without being asked Mr. Dith informs us, 'Clearing by the Yao for next year's crops.' A couple of times we pass spots where the fires have run down the hillsides and reached the track. Again without any questions from us: 'No permission.' Mr. Dith states. The heat from these breakaways is intense, the smell strong. The road is momentarily blocked from view by smoke then as we struggle around a steep curve: 'The School,' Iain and I both shout in unison.

There it sits, its metal roof glistening in the sunlight. Whoa! This really is happening. How much we wish our Project supporters could experience this thrill, though perhaps not the next fifteen minutes or so. The overnight heavy rains have caused the creek in front of Phoujong to rise alarmingly. Mr. Dith suggests we off-load ourselves in case his truck is swept sideways. Unsteady on my dodgy knees I am assisted across the uncomfortably strong flow by Iain on one side and Chanthy on the other.

We trudge through the mud of the village, our arrival announced by barking dogs, which can smell a *falang* at a hundred metres or more and squawking chickens. A couple of pigs are enjoying themselves in a deep wallow. We slip-slide across the culvert and up the steepest part of the track. Here we are met by the workers from the building site and we all push, grunting and groaning, until at last the much-abused vehicle shakes the slick mud from its tyres and zooms the last few metres to a halt.

The grey cement block walls are almost completed. Only a couple of courses left to lay. The metal roof is fully intact. The timber roof fascia board is already in place. We all but skip inside, to be greeted by a fall in temperature of probably as much as five degrees. Above us the entire roof space is lined with the magic insulation. There are smiles all round. The men have moved their sleep-platform, which up to now has been under the plastic awning tied onto the side of the old school, to the luxury of this cool inside and they grin broadly as we josh them about getting soft.

Mr. Khong shakes our hands. Thongkhanh *nops*. Outside at the far end of the building the over-worked cement mixer gripes and shudders while in and out of the doors the children dash about. Some of the young girls are building their Lego-style' structures with discarded broken blocks. Except that... oh golly! Spiderman is here, pint-sized, but in full regalia.

There is much to be shown and admire as well as to discuss and plan. Including the loos that are now all but ready for their ceramic pie-dishes.

The

Spiderman and girls:
No need for Lego

inside walls of the School are yet to be constructed and we must also discuss the need for cabling. Electricity has been promised to Phoujong, literally for years. Perhaps the building of The School will give that Government Department a kick in the posterior and get things moving. We need to be prepared for that by putting in place the wiring for fans and lighting in both classrooms as well as in the Teacher's

Almost finished loos

Room and the Teacher's Storeroom.

At the mention of this Mr. Khong looks somewhat embarrassed and it is explained to us that he has made a mistake in the initial diggings and there is no footing for the interior wall between the storage room and the Teacher's office.

'Bo peng yang' Iain assures him. No worries mate. Just build an interior wooden cavity wall with a lockable door in it. Mr. Khong's relief is apparent. Iain tells him again what a splendid job he is doing and that we are mightily impressed with the speed with which The School is being built, the non-stop hard work of his team of men and the quality of their work.

Builder Khong lets us know that he also needs cabling and switching materials for lights and fans brought down from LPB. After the awkwardness over the insulation material we had anticipated some resistance to putting in the necessaries for this yet-to-happen facility. But no such antipathy arose.

'You should also check out colours and costs of

wall and timber paint,' he suggests. 'Interior should be white. But the outside can be any colour you like. And don't forget undercoat too.'

Wall paint?! Extraordinary. Were we already approaching the stage of painting walls?!

Before leaving we pay Thongkhanh his salary plus extras for additional expenses. Thongkhanh immediately returns the envelope to us, saying 'Please give it to Bouchanh so she can put it in the bank.'

We arrange for Mr. Dith to pick us up at Teacher Kaojien's house in the village. Teacher Kaojien has gone into 'town', meaning Muang Nan, we are told, which is good because I am hoping to have time alone with his wife, her sister and their embroidery, as once again I have a plan bubbling in my mind. As it turns out we have no such luck because the father of Phoujong Headman Laisiew's Deputy, Gaojien (you managed to follow that did you?!) attaches himself to us as we try to saunter casually down the hill to the teacher's house. It doesn't help that this man is inebriated.

I have spent an entire day while we were on our recent stay in LPB reading a large format book replete with photographs, about the Yao, their history, culture, and customs including the importance of their embroidery. I had flicked through this particular book on previous visits while we were enjoying cool drinks on the riverside patio of The Belle Rive hotel.

Now it had become of intense interest to me and the young Swiss/German General Manager, Damien Killer, very kindly let me sit in the hotel's air-conditioned lobby and soak up its information so as to be better informed when I present my idea to Merynguen, Teacher Kaojien's wife.

Embroidery I had come to realize is to the Yao what Desert Art has become to the Aboriginal people of Central Australia. It is an expression of their culture and nothing less than a lifeline that anchors them in their very unsteady world.

As well as telling their Origin Story their embroidery is what sets them apart from the other myriad ethnic groups in the vast geographical areas across which they are now spread. It's a form of glue as it immediately identifies the wearer's background to other Yao as well as to other people. Fortunately the embroidery, as I had been privileged to witness, is even more portable than the hand-woven materials, rich with intricate designs, that are created by women from many other ethnicities and which require, for the most part, the use of back-strap looms. This portability has meant Yao women have carried their skills with them over many decades and across a series of borders.

But there are other demons that alienate hearts from beautiful handicrafts; chief amongst these is affluence. At the end of the American/VietNam war when literally hundreds of thousands of people from small ethnicities fled revenge, eventually to the USA, families who remained stranded in the mountain fastnesses of these remote areas found they were able to supplement their hand to mouth existence by selling their exquisite craftwork to their compatriots in the USA. These refugees were becoming wealthy by Lao standards and most certainly wealthy enough to purchase what they yearned for: memories of their Homeland.

Embroidered trousers such as the ones Merynguen had revealed to me fetched thousands of dollars from homesick Yao who had settled mostly in California but also around Seattle in Washington State. For the first decades after the great exodus there was a substantial cross Pacific trade in Yao embroideries. Every Yao woman who could afford to bought a pair of these to wear at her wedding, to a fellow Yao. Jackets, belts, caps, all elaborately embroidered with forgotten stories in traditional colours were similarly in high demand.

But fickle youth has put an end to all this. Many from this present generation view such costumes as just that, costumes and as such belonging to a theatre of a past from which they want to move on. Their desire to 'fit-in' to be 'accepted' in the culture into which they were born means saying No to these embroideries even though no doubt it breaks their Mother's hearts.

Trousers such as those Merynguen has embroidered and treasures as a link with her culture have been snapped up by the wealthy patrons of big museums and art galleries across the USA. They have become literally pieces of art to be viewed under low lights, to protect their fragility, in glass cabinets.

Where we could fit into all this ferment of sad history I was not at all sure. Just that my heart told me that hanging on to this talent, encouraging it in the next generation was as vital for Yao self-respect and survival as Emily Kingwayere's paintings are to her people.

My first thought was to buy at least one small piece, sell it to a like-minded soul in Australia and put the money back into the community of women in Phoujong for them to use as they saw fit; perhaps to buy more embroidery materials. Empowerment. Perhaps I could then mine deep enough among my contacts in the Australian Domestic Arts and Design world to uncover someone crazy enough to run with such a project and help it grow. Women as everyone realizes are the keepers of the stories: the saviours of their people's culture. Such a project would be a win/win.

But it was not to be.

Perhaps it would have been different if Gaojien's Dad had not been on the turps and insisted on joining in the conversation. Perhaps not, because it also has to be said that Merynguen had never once come up to the School even though her son was studying there; at least not when we were there. Nor even later did she attend the Opening. She never showed any interest in the Project even in support of her teacher husband. This could have been because of something personal between them or it could have been the result of some broader spread of cultural angst. There is no way we are going to get anywhere close to coming to grips with why. But that doesn't make it less disappointing.

Also perhaps because we had no common language, leaving me unable to explain to Merynguen, through Chanthy, the broader concept behind why I wanted to purchase a piece of her work, she rejected my suggestion and financial offer out of hand. She was very deliberate, very determined and I knew to back off. So I did, though I still have dreams of framing a piece of her embroidery to hang on a classroom wall in the School at Phoujong as a symbol of respect that would perhaps encourage some of the female students to continue her work in the years to come. I have another dream; multicoloured in red, black, white, green and blue of course, of bringing a display of her work along with that of other Yao embroiderers to show at our magnificent local Tweed

Regional Art gallery. We do after all share the same area of the world and anyway dreams are important; in fact they are vital

During that night the rain comes down thick and heavy again.

Merynyuen displays her embroidery flanked by her son and mother.

12 MONEY...MONEY...MONEY

...it's a rich man's world. Is it? Did Abba have it right? Or is that just another of life's illusions. We can talk about all this another time, but not right now because right now we really are at risk of completely running out of money. Not good. Very stress-inducing.

We knew before we left Australia, having sent the monies, depleted by the drop in the Australian dollar, ahead to Chanthy's account, that it would be a stretch to get the whole Project finalised. But sometimes you just have to leap in, boots and all. Faith. If we had waited any longer there was the very real possibility seasonal rains would have obliterated any possibility of building The School this calendar year. Putting matters off for a further twelve months, in the hope of raising more funds at home, is not a good choice at our age. We are already pushing the envelope. In addition who knows how far the Aussie dollar will continue to drop? There is also the crumbling knee to consider plus a second knee replacement planned for later in the year. From too close experience I know it's a fact that the outcome of major surgery is always an unknown. So we felt that it was now or never.

No doubt if you are a careful, planning style of character you will view this as irresponsibility. We see it as positive thinking and we did have some reasoning as backup because we were still telling ourselves that our application for funding from the Australian Government remained a distinct possibility.

For last year's project, the sixteen culverts on the Road to NaLin and on up to Phoujong, we had successfully applied for $5000 from the Direct Aid Programme. The DAP is an excellent scheme because it operates almost completely outside Australia's overall Foreign Aid budget which of itself is so miserly as to be embarrassing. Fortunately embassies in LDCs (Least Developed Countries) have a separate in-country fund dispersed at the discretion of the individual Ambassador with minimal recourse to Canberra. It is supervised by local staff who naturally have a far better handle on the on-ground situation.

The previous September Iain had filled in the necessarily complex application forms for further funding; this time for a School for Phoujong which surely had more immediate sex appeal than sixteen concrete culverts. So we were pretty positive about getting the money, though of course one should never count your chickens before they hatch and even with any extra Embassy funding there was no guarantee we'd have enough. Now, here we are five months later, more than anxious that our chickens could be coming home to roost. (Why this emphasis on chickens?)

An additional stress factor is that DAP monies are required to be spent on the approved project within the Australian financial year in which the dollars are given. So any monies now gifted will need to be spent before fast approaching June. As yet there had been no official yea or nay so we had metaphorically bitten our nails down to the quick and were even starting to question ourselves as well as each other about our can-do positive thinking.

The morning a brief email from Australian Consul and Second Secretary Jodie Rogers arrived saying she was happy to inform us that our application for funding had been approved, we were so delighted we celebrated by going to our trusted Vietnamese hardware shop and purchasing good quality, Chinese-made shutter and door fittings.

Unfortunately our exuberance was premature because though Ms. Rogers's email stated our application had been successful the actual readies still didn't appear in Chanthy's account, even though we knew the people at the Embassy had the relevant details.

Is this a case of 'the cheque is in the mail?' A distressed phone call from Dao Midgeley certainly makes us think this is a possibility. Dao too is waiting anxiously for funding for yet another school she and Stephen have built. They are using their own as well as their supporters' monies to keep things jogging along. When she tells us she hasn't even received a preliminary email from Jodie as we have, we feel even more anxious for them.

'I am going to send out an alms bowl email to everyone,' I tell rather than suggest to Iain. He has always felt that its preferable not to actually ask for money from people but rather to let them know what is happening and leave it up to them to hopefully not feel pressured but to put into the kitty of their own choice. No doubt his softly, softly approach is more appreciated than my more abrasive style. So between us, over the next few hours, we knock up an email that satisfies both our approaches and that we hope will empower our supporters to see the opportunity and want to help out.

Dear Penny and Richard

Since these photos were taken, the roof and insulation have been fitted, the main walls are well underway, the doors and windows are ready to install and work has started on the septic tank for the School's toilet block.

Roof beams up. Walls rising

With the roof up, the interior walls and floor are now being installed without major concern about the approaching rainy season.

Our funds have been holding up reasonably well so far, BUT, because we took a big hit with fall in the Aussie dollar...WE MAY NEED A LITTLE HELP.

(The A$28,000 raised in Australia fell to just a bit over US$21,000 when we transferred it to Laos)...so we lost A$7,000. We've had a contribution from the Oz

Embassy in Laos since, but we have some concern that things will be a little tight for the finishing off work on both the school itself and in particular, the building of the septic toilet block and its plumbing. There's also the rendering and painting of both buildings as well as a rainwater collection system. So, if you feel inspired to add a little extra contribution towards finishing the Phoujong School project, the details of how to do it are sent separately.

When the School is finished, anything left over from extra funds collected, will go towards installing electric wiring, fans and lights in the School. Even though the village still has no electricity, they are expecting it within a year or so, but if we can have the school ready for it, we won't have to retrofit it later. Also there's a need for decent desks and seats in the school, and of course books.

In addition, depending on what funds are available, the school at NaLin village, some five kilometres away, needs around US$4,000 to $5,000 spent on replacing a rotting ceiling, so its not as if there's a shortage of worthwhile projects.

Everything here is happening so fast!...many ignorant people dismiss the Lao as lazy/non-motivated....well... they should watch 'our crew' in action. I am filled with admiration ... I want to hug every one of them...but I restrain myself. More lessons in self-restraint! Hugging not the go!

All they need...like everyone...is someone to believe in them. To show confidence in them. Perhaps that is love in one of its many guises. Love...by the by...as a word...is also not the go. As always I am learning SO much. The three way chats we have...with Chanthy as man-in-the-middle...are so revelatory. They ask us about Australia of course...as well as our families...and even...why we are doing this! Explaining to outsiders how systems in your own country operate is a good way of learning...about your own country! As well as understanding the similarities (most) and dissimilarities (least)...is very educative...and at this grass-roots level...so very informative.

We have so many laughs through conversations over 'lunch' of spicy buffalo laap *and sticky rice...eaten with fingers...under the smoke-filled flapping tarpaulin...with the students watching our every mouthful...and the dog waiting for droppings...during one Mr. Khong and Mr.Thongkhanh suggested that any insulation material that is left-over after the job is completed should be used to make jackets! to keep out the heat...they will employ city-slicker Chanthy to design what young people would like! The ladies of the village with their antique Singer sewing machine can run them up...and Jai can take them up to Luang Prabang on his clapped out motorbike to sell in the Night Market to cashed up falang! Everyone chortles. The heat is INTENSE...and they quickly* overcame any hesitation they had about our rolls of insulation...when the difference ...under the tin roof... was so immediately apparent. The word quickly spread...and now outside people visit the site to marvel! and even people down at District Centre Muang Nan know of the miracle material.

We have our morning pho-pak *(veg/noodle soup)* at the tiny family-run caff beside where the small buses pull-up. Of course the lady who owns the shop...and indeed her whole family...now know us and what is happening in Phoujong...and they often sit with us and eat...Here we re-met the Noodle Lady (for those of you who have read my Road to NaLin book!)...and came to understand her full business acumen...selling noodles on the early morning run down from Luang Prabang...and...tiny frogs on the way back up! Clever her!

Chanthy bought a bag of the still jumping amphibians ...salivating over how he would cook them in his room... only eating the legs AND the head...not...he assured us... the guts...and then regaled us with stories of his childhood pre-dawn expeditions into the rice paddies with his Father to catch smallish rodents by pulling them from their burrows and of course getting nipped by their sharp teeth. That was in the dry season when the paddies were filled with last season's dry stalks. In the wet they went for frogs...wearing small torches tied to their heads. Frogs eyes reflect light. But you had to be careful.   O n e eye could mean the frog was looking ahead rather than straight at you. But the reflection from a single eye could also mean it was a snake! Or...just as poisonous...a spider. This was not a father/son bonding tree-hugging expedition! This was an essential food-gathering event. Chanthy is a natural born storyteller and everyone laughs...as indeed he laughs himself.

Of course the people here all have the same complications we all have in our family and non-family relationships.

On is waiting for her second child to be born. It is ten days overdue. Everyone...including us... is nervous... but this is not expressed as such. Buachanh is home from the burial rites for her brother ...the burning of the body the scraping clean of the bones...the placing of these into a sealed jar...and the building in the forest of the small stupa into which this jar has been placed.

Thongkhanh has made a one-day visit by motorbike to support his cousin through decisions over his cousin's son's divorce. Not a simple matter...financially or emotionally... And Chanthy is dealing with his first full-on romantic attachment. His mother sends up little plastic bags of chicken and mushrooms by bus for him to make nurturing soup! Ah mothers! What to do with them... what to do without them!

Headman Dith's father has been sent home from hospital to die. He has bowel cancer. Pain killers are at a premium. Dith's eldest child...a daughter ...wants to train *as a nurse...and is very focused...his other child...a son... has no plans for his future...and I try to cheer Dith up by telling stories out of school about our own 18 year old grandson's similar lack of self-discipline...at which they all laugh with a parental knowingness.*

Bounlee's husband (Mr. Khong's son) is working on all his off-duty times at the building site. He is a high-school teacher...but government pay is extremely irregular...so he works steadily, with quiet determination...beside his father...who obviously invests great trust in him...because he gives him important jobs... and then leaves him to get on with it...

On the weekend the Yao people from Phoujong village filled in what will be the schoolroom floors with soil...soon to be covered with a reinforced concrete slab . They are becoming more at ease with us. After all it must be difficult for them to understand why we are doing this! We have explained that we are just the front people for a team of a hundred at home and elsewhere in the world that simply want to make a difference for the better. The Yao are so accustomed to being kicked around at the bottom of the social pile...as happens in every society... that they have an inbuilt suspicion...as a protection mechanism...but non-teeth-exposing smiles! and non-asking, non-questioning behaviour on our part goes a long way towards being accepted.

Digging the pit for the septic tank

The villagers also did all the backbreaking sweat-inducing job of digging the deep pits for the latrines. Aaaah latrines! Imagine that! What will they think of next!

The bus drivers up and down on Route 12 give us smiles of recognition. We wend along through the annual burn-off that clouds the skies and tears at the eyes. The Tweed Valley burn is nothing compared with this! We rattle up and down high mountains through teak forests and rubber plantations... and oh yes...the Chinese...again I meant to leave room to tell you about this ... as it is in fact THE single most important deal...but I have let myself go yammering on once more...but I promise...next time!

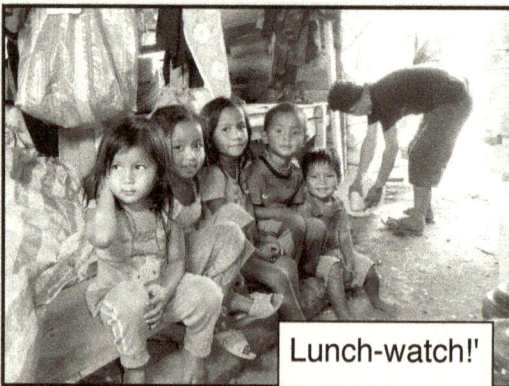

Lunch-watch!'

Meanwhile... thank you for making all of this possible. You are making an important *and BIG difference for the better.   Big hugs...   trish*

Sending this email to more than a hundred people, along with an accompanying all-important individual note to each, is exhausting because of the draw on emotions and also because of the frustrations of a wobbly Internet connection that comes and goes. But looking at this photograph that I attach at the end of each email spurs me on.

It also makes me realise that if I was, due to a mere accident of birth, in the situation most Phoujongers are in, I fear I might not be able to move on from deep anger. I would more than likely behave in ways that perhaps indeed would be non-productive. I would probably not be able to accept my unequal lot in life and the uncaring world. I might in fact be very dangerous.

Somewhat snuffed by the hours-long strenuous struggles with the small screen we decide that an early night might be the go, only to find that my overworked brain keeps me awake with anxieties about whether in some way or other we had been too forthright in our request for help and whether we had unwittingly stepped on the toes of the keeper of the monies for the DAP funding.

The following morning, as is so often the way with these things, there is an email from Ms. Mouth asking for the name of the account into which she can deposit the DAP funds. By return Iain emails the details of the Road to NaLin bank account that we had opened the year before last. In the hope of speeding things along he also calls the Embassy and Ms. Mouth informs him that the Road to NaLin account won't do. There has to be a new account, the name of which has to be: *The Phoujong Primary School and Toilet Facility.*

So off to the bank with Chanthy, remembering to take passports, to establish this unusually named bank account followed by another phone call to Ms. Mouth giving her the accounting number and other details, but she of course has to wait for official advice from the bank itself.

It is difficult to put all these money matters far enough to one side to be able to think about other things, so its fortunate indeed that on returning to our guesthouse we are met by the owner, who has been away in Vientiane.

What we both immediately notice about Taykeo Sayavongkhamdy is her *sin*, the traditional calf-length Lao wrap over skirt that all Lao women wear though, despite Government edicts, its omniscience is somewhat under threat among the younger generation who naturally prefer to experiment with world-wide clothing trends and to wear jeans and even shorts.

Taykeo's *sin* is much more than a skirt; it is a piece of art. She is pleased we comment so favourably about it and assures us that it is at least fifty years old. The entire skirt, from waist to hem, is made of hand-woven silk; not delicate fine silk but gorgeous thick twisted multi-threads made into intricate geometric patterns created in natural hues.

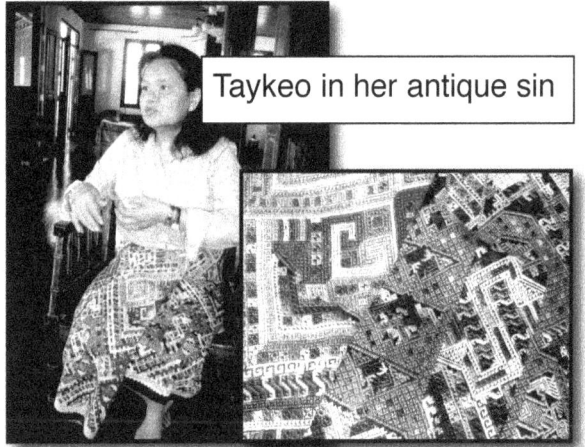

Taykeo in her antique sin

'You must visit my textile gallery in Vientiane,' she insists. 'We are training young women in the old arts that are in danger of dying out. We grow our own silkworms, spin our own silk, use natural dyes made from bark and flowers and weave our own cloth using traditional methods. The results are very beautiful but there is something even more special about antique textiles. It is as if they have a story of their own to tell. Some of my old pieces were lost during the Change of Government, but I managed to hold on to a sizeable collection.'

Taykeo sees the light in my eyes and senses my interest. Of course I am daydreaming about the imaginary Textile Showing at the Tweed Art Gallery, which incidentally had just been placed fourth on the listing of most excellent Galleries of Australia. Taykeo says 'Whenever I wear this *sin* overseas women stop me in the street to comment on its beauty,' I believe her because I know its true that in these instant pleasure, then throwaway times, people still respond to deeper beauty.

We come to understand that when Taykeo talks about 'overseas' she is referring to Australia. She and her husband, Thongsa Sayavongkhamdy, one of, if not the, nation's leading archaeologists, have three sons and a daughter. All of them were awarded scholarships to study in Australia and we are to meet them all, also their father, at the rapidly approaching Pi Mai festivities. Having all of them graduated with honours only one of them, son Saybandith, has returned to Laos. He is now Deputy Director of the Multilateral Trade Division in the Ministry of Industry and Commerce Foreign Trade Policy Department. This mouthful of a title is unfortunately not commensurate with the salary he earns in his Homeland. He could certainly earn a sizeable amount more in Australia. But when, later on, we get to converse with him he enthuses over the future of Laos and his part in it. 'If not me,' he says, 'then my daughters.'

Mekong Charm guesthouse is a sideline for Taykeo. The family, in Australia and Laos, clubbed together a few years back to buy a rundown Mekong riverside block of land. Very good move. As Laos frees itself from political shackles and increasingly engages with the world of market forces the value of the land cannot do other than increase exponentially in value, along with the guesthouse they have built on it.

A few days later, as a follow-up to our interest in Taykeo's textiles she arranges for a young woman to come in from one of the outlying villages to show us her handicraft. This is something else again. Gold thread that had been intricately woven and embroidered into sets of heavy cuffs and collars to be worn on very special celebratory occasions such as weddings. So much talent. So much beauty. It has to be preserved.

Having forced ourselves to give the bank time to breath we pop by there just before closing time and

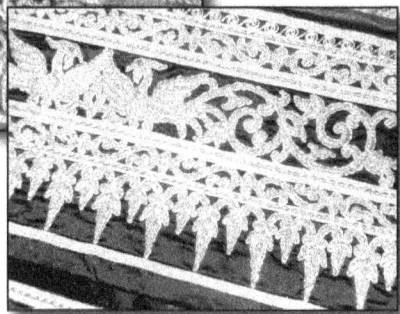

are informed that yes, the dollars from the Australian Embassy have been deposited. All 10,000 of them. Ten thousand, but we only applied for five. How come? Should we point out this doubling of fortune?

We discuss this moral dilemma while having a celebratory meal of fried chicken from the KFC next door to our guesthouse. KFC!?! Yes, well, just kidding...a Lao version! And much better for that. We don't eat meat, not even chicken but we feel we should support the hard-working owner of this street stall.

We are generally awoken just before dawn every day by the chopping of wood, the setting of a cooking fire and the clatter of metal pots, coming from the alleyway running along below the side window of our room. While getting ready to take off on our rented bicycles we take sneak looks down at this industrious woman as she puts a very large container of water on the fire and when it is boiling tips in large numbers of frozen chicken wings and thigh-bones. By the time we leave, as the sky over the Mekong is lightening, these chicken pieces that we later learn have been bought in bulk from Thailand, have been defrosted and she is patting down each piece of flesh and carefully storing them in large plastic containers, ready for the next stage of culinary preparation.

This occurs at close-on four every afternoon, at

which time Iain is usually still sitting at his computer, while I am attempting to relax on our balcony with my knitting and she is setting up her kerbside eatery. Dipping the pre-boiled chicken pieces into a tub of flour, frying them up in an oiled wok, lying them on paper to drain, sprinkling them with spices and serving them to a constant stream of customers who stop by on their motorbikes or even in Government cars. All this is achieved while supervising her older children who sit on the step behind her doing their school homework

as well as comforting her smallest child, a very demanding three-year-old daughter.

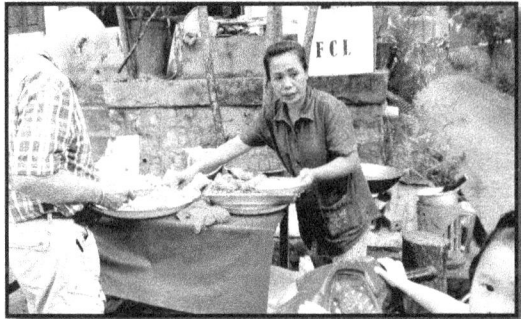

KFC Laos style

Her constant patience and determined hard work would be sufficient to impress us but what really knocks our sox off is when Chanthy introduces us to her as Thiphavun, his IT teacher from the business college where he is studying. This means that her early morning par-boiling of chicken bits, plus running this stall, seven afternoons a week, is only her part-time job! She does this on top of teaching full-time every day and, of course, looking after her children. Her husband, Chanthy tells us, is away down south, employed by the army and is only able to come back home every month of so.

So this is why we buy some chicken legs from Thiphavun and sit alongside her stall to munch on them while watching the fishing and trading craft on the river and talking over the unexpected doubling of our monies!

13 YOU DID IT!

The response to our email was instantaneous, very generous and completely did away with the fears we had that we had gone too far in asking directly for help.

Thank you to everyone who came good.

We want to say a special thank you to Ged and Denise Brotherton not because theirs was the largest donation, in fact it wasn't, but because we know them well enough to be aware

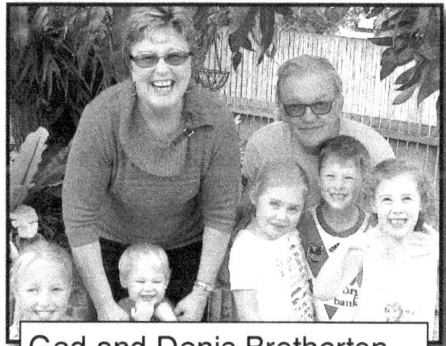

Ged and Denis Brotherton with their five grandchildren

that they have an average wage, so the monies they sent were not 'spare'; they were earned the hard way.

Ged and Denise, who both work for Queensland Rail, stipulated that they wanted their donation spent on new school uniforms for the Phoujong students. We are doubly grateful for this because we'd had uniforms on our wish list but due to the shortfall in funds it had not seemed feasible. Now we had the earmarked kip.

Then, we sent the following email out to everyone... not only those who had topped up the account.

PHUJONG SCHOOL......AND LOO!!!!

We're into the home straight now...and going for the

finishing line!

THANK YOU. All of you for that vital last input!

No more $$ needed.

Been a bit of a nail-biter! But I guess we live at our best out here on the edge!

We have always known and respected the fact that the two of us are simply the pointy-end instigators...making this Project become a reality for others...and we see this as a special privilege.

One person made a donation because they had experienced first-hand the horror of their personal funds being massacred by a vicious drop in the foreign exchange rate.

While very longtime friends...a couple...with a grandchild...are such committed hard-workers that they can't bring themselves to take time-out for a holiday... and view our Project as vicarious armchair travels!

Another made a sizeable donation...to honour a family bereavement.

Over the five plus years we have been at this we have been consistently surprised and touched by how it has sewn people together in a totally unexpected but beautiful patchwork quilt of life.

How's this for instance. When I was at boarding

school I had two special mates. The terrifyingly bright one went on to become a very big wheel in the British Intelligence Service...holding down the equivalent rank of General. The other, very cluey and personable, went on to co-establish a large and extremely successful land and building development company on the west coast of America. We are now of an age that was unimaginable back then when we met on the brink of our adult lives. We have stayed in touch over the decades and they have both made very sizeable contributions to this Project. I like that. Because it feels as if we have woven a bright thread together into this fragile tapestry we describe as Life!

The reason for all this soppy introspection is because we are coming pretty close to a wrap!

I LOVE MY LOO!

This is the penultimate email from the Project: a School for Phoujong.

After this...one more week...and we have to go home...

...to have something done that I can't put off any longer: a total knee replacement! I know, I know...these ops are so common they pass without comment nowadays! That's true. As long as it isn't you that's having the op!

Everyone here has been so patient with this hobbling old lady...helping me up and down from vehicles and over obstacles...while of course no one has been intrusive enough to inquire as to why this is so...that's just not the Lao way...so when the time came that I had to explain why we were having to go home...I chose NaLin Headman Mr. Dith to spill the beans to...and I am so glad I did... because he LAUGHED! He did! Out loud! And then he laughed some more...at my explanations of a 'new knee' that included wild hinge-ing motions... Over time Mr. Dith has become special to me...probably because he gets my oblique jokes! and naturally he thought this was simply one of those! Well it is preposterous when viewed from his life-experience...to hack a leg open, chop out worn-out bits... stuff in some plastic/metal pieces...sew it all up and expect it to work. He's heard of false teeth! And he's even inspected Iain's hearing aids! But a false knee!! That took the prize!! He laughed even after he realised I was being

235

serious!

'Falang!' I could hear him thinking. 'They build a road. They put in culverts. They even choose the most difficult situation around here in which to build a school. And now...a False Knee!!...' We laughed together at the outrageiosity of it! And if that isn't a word...it should be! We chuckled all the way back down the track to town... with occasional inserts of laughter...and I will be carrying his response with me to the operating room... hoping it will help me through!

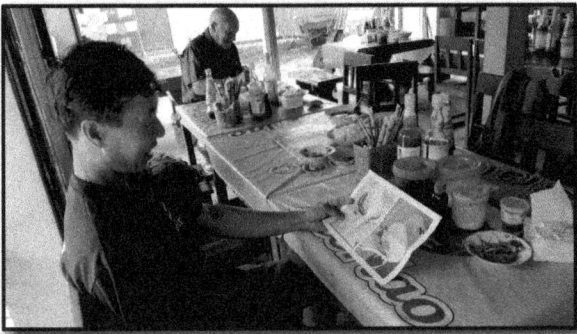

Mr. DITH CHUCLES OVER AN ILLUSTRATION OF MY UP-COMING KNEE OP at our favourite noodle shop in Muang Nan.

Thongkhanh came up on the bus with us...to visit a doctor...who diagnosed a severe stomach/gut infection... and filled him up with antibiotics and antispasmodics. Thongkhanh is nothing if not stoic. Too stoic. From habit born of need. Whereas Mr. Dith originally trained as a soldier...and then as a policeman...Thonghkhanh trained as a teacher...but when neither man was paid a regular wage...they returned to doing what they knew best would *at least feed their families...rice-farming. We have stressed to Thongkhanh that he must finish the complete course of antibiotics...and not stop halfway through... even if he starts to feel better. And we have tried to suggest he could give his stomach a rest from spicy food... and meat....even going so far as to mention giving up the smokes. But of course none of this is about to happen!*

Builder Khong has announced that he will have The School completed in time for Pi Mai...Lao New Year... which begins on the 14th April. That means he has come in on time...and on budget!!!!!!!!

Woohoo! how often have you heard of that happening with a building project?!

The intensity of expectation about Pi Mai is HUGE! Street parades and parties...elephants...apsaras (angels) ...water guns...food stalls...and rather a lot of highly potent Lao-lao...the toffs in their finery and the rest just out to have fun. It is a magic time for kids. And at this time of year everyone becomes a kid. Ms. Pi Mai Beauty Contest (no bathing suits!)...the most sacred of Buddha images...the Jade Buddha...being processed along the main street. The newly shaven heads of monks and novices glistening in the burdensome sun and the 4.30am drummings from the 33 wats, all seemingly louder than ever.

Already water is being sloshed over the unwary. The symbolism of washing out the old year and bringing in a sparkly new year is obvious.

CATCHING OUT THE UNWARY...IN THE MAIN
ROAD OF DISTRICT CENTRE MUANG NAN.

The rains have held off. But the earlier worrying drenchings have raised the level of the Mekong to the extent that the sand-bank/island that is usually...at this time of year... above water mid-river just offshore from town...is still submerged. Because this is where a great amount of the jollity occurs and where sand-stupas are built and adorned with spectacular prayer flags...the Government in true Lao style!...is planning on dredging sand from elsewhere and building up the sand-island! in time for Pi Mai...and ready for it all to be washed away. A bit like New Year fireworks over Sydney Harbour! wasteful but symbolic and therefore very important.

The paint has been chosen and bought. The school uniforms purchased. The rendering is going on apace. The shutters and doors going in. The wonder of the roof insulation and its cooling effect remains a source of amazement. There are books to buy....a festivity has been planned by the Phoujong community....and we have managed to politely suggest that buffalo is not required!

We shall of course let you know how all this goes... and keep you in the loop so as you can wallow in these joys!

Kopchai!

trish/iain

Rather sadly, on the bus back down to Muang Nan, we 'lost' our extra $5000! We mentioned our 'bonus win' to Chanthy. He immediately looked somewhat embarrassed before explaining the sum was more than likely the amount that the villagers of NaLin had applied for to the Australian Embassy because they were anxious to have their school repaired. This had been built five years previously, with funding from a Japanese NGO, but unfortunately incorrect timber had been used in constructing its ceilings and this had resulted in full-on attacks by termites. It had now reached the stage where the flaking timbers fell like a continuous snowstorm onto the heads and shoulders of the young students.

Obviously we couldn't begrudge NaLin pupils a replacement ceiling but we were a bit non-plussed that neither Chanthy nor anyone else in the village had thought to tell us of their application.

'We planned to wait until we heard from Ms. Mouth and when we didn't we thought it wasn't going to happen,' Chanthy explained. Fair enough. Then Iain looked like a light bulb had been switched on inside his head as he went swiftly from being slightly miffed to seeing the upside.

'Its fine Chanthy,' he said, 'in fact its great. It is precisely what we wanted to happen. This is how it should be. You, or at least the villagers, have seen how the DAP system works, so from now on you can apply for monies and we can stay behind the scenes and just be there to help guide things along.' At the time we had no idea how this would work but in fact it is what has happened

Buying uniforms in Muang Nan market

In Muang Nan our first stop is the all-day market where we surprise, and no doubt delight, a young woman stallholder by requesting thirty-five school uniforms in Primary pupil sizes. Naturally she doesn't have enough stock on hand but assures us she will top up supplies by asking around among her fellow stallholders. Several mobile phone calls are made between Chanthy, Teacher Kaojien and the stallholder to ascertain how many boys and how many girls and what sizes to get.

There are several building suppliers around town whose final bills we need to pay and there are numerous extra five-litre cans of both flat white and flat yellow paint plus a couple of gorgeous garnet coloured full-gloss ones to pick up. We had chosen the paint from a colour chart at the small hardware outlet before going up to Luang Prabang. The choice had been easy to make because there was a simple one-page list showing a few very basic colours. We had settled on yellow, because all Government schools are an unimaginative white. Foolishly I tell Chanthy that in Australia the choice of paint colours includes over one hundred shades of white and he smiles at what he takes to be my joke. It is one of the very few occasions on which Chanthy misunderstands me. This is the man who always gets my sideways, throwaway remarks more quickly than do many English-speaking friends at home. But of course how could he possible be expected to imagine the over-the-top paint colour charts at our local Bunnings where among the myriad of possible tones and colours there is no such thing as just simple white paint and instead there truly are over one hundred shades of white.

His non-understanding of this not being a casual jokey remark focuses my mind. From experience over a

241

half decade I now know that if there is anything I feel I cannot explain to Chanthy, this indicates it is too trivial to be worthy of commenting on to anybody. I have come to understand that by some unrealized process of osmosis Chanthy, with his uncomplicated view of life, has become a vital reference point for me on what is important and what is not. Would he be surprised if I told him this? Most likely not.

We also stop by the Education Department Office on the edge of town and lock in a date for an Official Opening. September 1st, the first day of the new Laos school year, is settled on for the event and is even carefully marked in a desk diary. At this time four months seems a long way off but it turns out to be so dense with happenings that it was another example of the elasticity of time. The astounding fact is that it is only eight weeks since we were in this same office, with assorted villagers and the building crew, signing off on plans to start building a School for Phoujong!

The following morning Mr. Dith comes by the Saylomgnen Guest House to collect us for the final run, for this visit, up the Hadsaikham River Valley in his battered Hyundai. During the days we have been away the gearbox of this much-abused vehicle had more or less disintegrated When Chanthy had told us this we had decided that the Project should take responsibility for its repair because without it and Mr. Dith being on immediate call, we would not have been able to make the many bone-jarring journeys up and down to Phoujong. We asked Chanthy to find out what the repairs had cost and were told it was almost $100, inclusive of fitting. When we give this amount to Mr. Dith he is genuinely delighted, saying this the first time in his life anyone has ever given him money without him asking, and having to wait, for it We try explaining that this would be how things would happen in an Australian workplace situation in which people use their private cars for work-related journeys. He happily gives us the receipt from the mechanic's shop.

We pack up the back of the truck with the extra cans of paint plus paint brushes with long handles that Iain has assured Thongkhanh will make the big job of painting all the walls, inside and out, a great deal easier. We also squeeze in the tricycle, bought with our own monies, as a gift for Sydney from an outlet in Luang Prabang and again transported by the tolerant bus driver. Sometimes I think that if we had asked him to stow a baby elephant in his baggage compartment he would have agreed without so much as a blink.

Mr. Dith then runs the gauntlet of a number of over-excited early Pi Mai water throwers, though he uses the elderly *falang* woman in the front seat as an excuse to dissuade one teenaged girl from turning her gigantic water hose on us.

Fortunately with have had the foresight to stash the thirty-five school uniforms in the cabin with us. This makes the space for Chanthy even more ridiculously cramped, but off we go.

There have been a few heavy though thankfully short showers, precursors of what is inevitably to come. The surfaced road to the edge of town glistens with a slight smear of slippery mud and there is a small delay when a large water buffalo lumbers towards us as if intent on charging the vehicle only to turn away at the last moment like a teasing matador.

After less than ten kilometres, travelling between the rice paddies, we do a left turn off onto a the dirt road that wends through attractive plantations of teak and other tropical trees to reach the small riverbank village of Hadsaikham and the compact woodworking workshop of Mr. Sengchan and his business partner and fellow carpenter, Mr. Bountheung. We are keen to see how work is progressing here to build all the doors and windows for the school.

The two them had visited the school worksite ten days or so previously to talk about preparations for the six timber doors and eleven sets of window frames, plus shutters that have been a part of the plan since building began. At the meeting there had been plenty of happy banter while sizes and prices were discussed. It was all very open. Other tradesmen came and went and a few of the students, girls and boys, sat around on the battered wooden benches to listen in. Nobody seemed to mind at all and I sat with them hoping that some of these bartering skills were being learnt and could be of use to the children later in their own working lives.

Negotiations completed, we agreed to be responsible for bringing down the necessary door and shutter hardware from LPB. 'Better to pay a little more and get good quality handles, locks, hinges and fasteners than go for the cheaper Chinese equivalent,' Sengchan told us, unconsciously echoing Australian tradies.

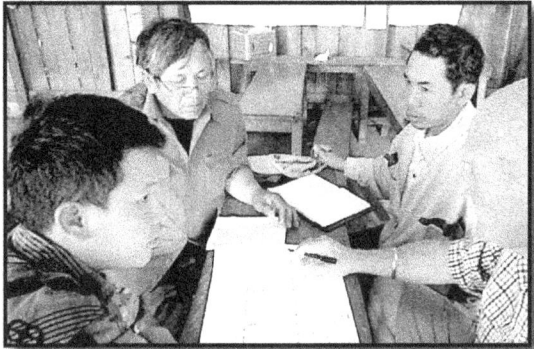

Sengchan & Bountheung discuss the carpentry work

During his visits to the School we had noticed that 54-year-old Sengchan didn't use fingers-full of sticky rice to scoop up the shared meal along with everyone else. Instead he brought food in a separate container though he eyed the building crew's meals with a sad longing. He told us he had recently been diagnosed with diabetes and the Lao staple of sticky rice, eaten morning, noon and night by everyone else, was now a no-go zone for him because it contained an excess of sucrose.

We have known Sengchan for some years because his home in NaLin is the nearest one to the Sisombuth's house; so close that they have what in western terms would be described as a shared front yard. This has meant that we have spent a deal of time with his family and over the years we have accrued quite a bit of knowledge about his personal history. During our stay the previous year we were honoured to be invited to a baci in his home held to celebrate the meeting of Sengchan and his sister for the first time since they had been separated as children during the American War

From earlier conversations we know that Sengchan fought with the Pathet Lao forces against the Americans and has a smashed leg as a legacy of this war. When Iain had rather awkwardly told him he himself had been a television journalist covering that nasty war for the other side Sengchan had shown no surprise, simply remarking, 'War is not how it appears on television.'

So as a survivor of teenaged years spent soldiering in the cauldron of the American fire-bombing of the Plain of Jars and the Ho Chi Minh Trail, in Lao's far eastern Xiengthong Province, Sengchan more than likely feels fortunate to have only a smashed leg as a legacy and to have survived long enough to have developed diabetes. Age is a very relative matter.

In the almost totally all-Lao village of NaLin Sengchan's wife, Ms.Lar, is a standout. She is the woman with whom I recently winnowed the family hops crop and she is Khmu. Darker of skin than those around her she would have been a knockout looker as a younger woman and now as a mature woman she glows with inner confidence.

More than likely because Sengchan's wife is from this minority group he and only he, from among all the villagers, has asked us how things are going between us, the School builders and the Yao and Hmong villagers of Phoujong. We of course diplomatically said 'we're all getting along just fine'. He had given a knowing nod and said, 'don't be surprised if sometimes there are difficulties.'

He is, as far as we have yet ascertained, the only tradesman in NaLin with his own workshop. From this very basic set-up he produces, with

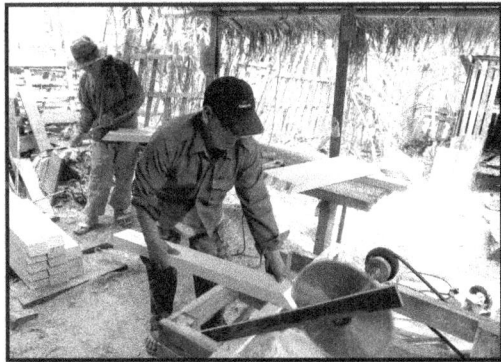

Sengchanh making window frames

the help of at least one apprentice, doors and window shutters of considerable beauty made from timber he collects, almost certainly without a permit, from the nearby forests.

Now he and Bountheung are busy making the last of the shutters for the School. I stand way back from the saw and sanding machines, none of which have safety guards and so are sending out great gushes of tinder-dry sawdust. The heat under the metal roof is brain frying. The floor is ankle deep in wood shavings. The smell of new timber is fragrant and Bountheung's wife brings us very welcome bottles of cold water. Their dog licks his chops as he watches us drink.

Fitting in the window and door frames

The men assure us they will be bringing the final batch of shutters up to the School that afternoon and we tell him that we will have their last payment ready to give them at that time.

We have also told Teacher Kaojieng we would like to bring the uniforms up to the School and film him giving them out to the children. As well we have also forewarned Mr. Khong and his building crew that we needed at least the front of the building finished because we want to film it and this will be our last opportunity before we have to leave.

Mr. Khong has made it all happen. The front of a School for Phoujong glows in all its soft yellow glory. The garnet doors and verandah edging set it off to perfection. I have never felt such a deep satisfaction, an at-peace-with-myself glow.

But there is no time at all for enjoying all these emotions. In fact it isn't until weeks, perhaps even months, later that the full impact of what has happened unrolls and knits itself into my being.

Right now we only have just enough time to admire the dirt floor that has been shoveled in by hand by the village men, then covered with a cement topping by the outside work crew, before the children of Phoujong charge up the hill to the old school. They have been induced by a promise from Iain of receiving the equivalent of twenty cents each if they assist in cleaning up the worksite.

They set to with cheerful good will, collecting discarded empty cement bags, broken cement blocks, small pieces of rubbish timber. Carrying and dragging these bits across to the side of the old school they dump them in a garbage pit the workers have dug and where now a slow burning fire swallows it all up. As they

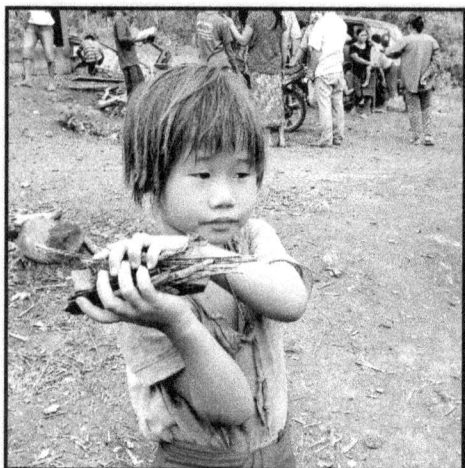

Rubbish cleanup

participate in this shared work–play, including Bounyang on his walker, they laugh and sing and call out to each other filling the air with that same sound children enjoying themselves make anywhere in the world. When the job is complete they line up, Iain doles out the small denomination kip notes and they leap, well the boys anyway, back down the hill to spend their well-earned wages buying up vile coloured lollies from the only 'shop' in the settlement

It is not long before they come streaming back up to the old school, full of anticipation, aware that the delights of the day are far from over. Under instructions from Teacher Kaojien and Chanthy they settle their little bodies, squirming with energy and anticipation, on battered benches at their much-used tables before the men begin to give out the uniforms from Ged and Denise. Most of these children would never have owned any piece of a school uniform and for those that have it would certainly have been a hand-me-down from an older sibling. None of them would have ever had a complete new outfit. It is not long before happy chaos breaks out. There are shy smiles and embarrassed giggles as unfamiliar shirt-buttons are fastened; over-long sleeves rolled and trouser legs hitched up as well as sins wrapped. Scruffy urchins

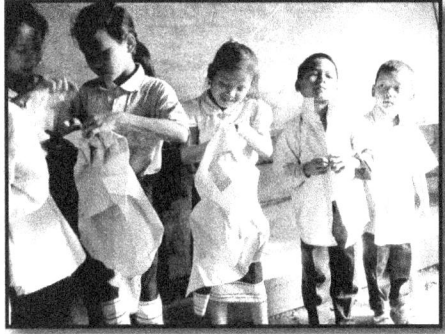

Students putting on their new uniforms

metamorphose into well-kempt students. Everyone gives everyone else admiring looks before realising they too have changed.

I have heard the conversation about uniforms being militaristic and therefore out of place in schools. But in this situation uniforms bring feelings of self-respect and self-worth along with that of sharing and belonging.

We have chosen not to purchase the red cotton Pioneer neckerchiefs that students in Lao cities and towns wear with their uniform. They are symbolic of the National Government and as such rather out of place in this struggling village that has for so long been overlooked.

I have also noticed that although Kaojien always wears a smart, clean khaki Education Department uniform he does not pin on the bright red shoulder tabs, insignia to which he is due and that would designate his rank. So we take our lead from his small gesture.

In the cooling afternoon we all go outside to stand in front of their new school, a School for Phoujong. This tiny moment is captured on film, frozen in time for future generations. The children wave. We all smile. It is done. It is well done.

But the rows of faces, all of whom we have become so familiar with over these past months look at us with a brightness that denotes they know this one-off day still has one last puff of wind in its sail.

At a word from Teacher Kaojien they rush off in a chattering mob, away to show their new school clothes to their families. We follow down the hill, at a far slower pace, reluctant to leave what for us has grown into what Australian Aboriginal people would designate, a Sacred Place. A spot on the earth where something very special happened.

***

We shake hands with and say our thanks to all members of the work crew and I even manage to get in a small hug with Mr. Khong. Everyone has been invited to attend the baci that is about to get underway in a home on the edge of the settlement; only the remarkable Thongkhanh accepts the gesture, along with his equally remarkable son Chanthy. Both of them have respectfully changed into clean shirts and long trousers and I wonder again at their ability, without any fuss, to be always prepared to be so present in the moment.

I would not be able to tell you whose home we enter, or where exactly in the village it is. If you told me that the events of the next half hour unfolded in a spaceship visiting from Mars I would not disbelieve you because the experience was so otherworldly.

What I can vividly recall is the close atmosphere in the dusky evening light, the crowd of bodies tightly packed into the room and the sound of an expectant hush.

In deference to our age, plus my incapacity, we are seated on small chairs close to the phakhoum the ceremonial flower tree, which someone with special hands has managed to bring to life, despite this being a drab, flowerless place. Silence spreads as morphon Tidniew begins a chanting to call in the spirits. This ability to meld into coherence the religious rites important to the mix of ethnicities in Phoujong village must be a challenge.

I am sorry that Mr. Khong and his work-crew are not here. It would have been a big goodwill gesture. The same applies to the absent Merynguyen, creator of spectacular embroidery and wife of Teacher Kaojien. But, I tell myself, you can never win them all and its still early days. Then in the dim light I spot Sanfin who at the beginning came unsettlingly close to unseating the whole project. The arm, that was so badly damaged in his spectacular car crash, is still in a supportive sling. We exchange small nods of reconciliation.

All these insignificant temporal thoughts fade away as Tidniew's chanting increases in speed and volume. We place our fingertips on the central platter bearing the phakhoum, aware as we do so that other people are touching our shoulders and backs to enable the flow of energy to pass through us and on to others. Humming vibrations eat the air before, for a split second there is a void, as if the world is holding its breath. The light dims perceptibly, and then just as speedily as it came, whatever it is, goes. The spell is broken. Everyone speaks at once and there is a shared sense of relief. It is as if we have been to the edge together and are glad to have all come back.

Tidniew flicks drops of Lao-lao into the air and then more drops over Iain and I before tearing pieces from the cooked chicken whose carcass had been wrapped around the base of the phakhoum. He offers these to us and after us to the other people in the inner ring. A shot-glass of Lao-lao is proffered to Iain who does as is expected of him, and drains it in one fast swill. There is a murmur of appreciation from the other men. Under cover of being a mere woman I politely decline a similar offer.

Then it is on for young and old as everyone crowds forward with small cut pieces of white cotton prayer strings to tie around our wrists while stroking us and murmuring good wishes. We give up any hope of filming this happening but without any request from us Thongkhanh, now totally tuned in to the needs of this odd *falang* couple, takes Iain's camera and captures the proceedings.

Teacher Kaojien brings his 6 year old son, Low, forward to present us with hard-boiled eggs the shells of which have been dyed a deep red. They are individually cradled in a lace of green yarn and he gently places one around each of our necks. I know that these coloured eggs are used in the Hmong New Year festivities and I am glad that they have managed to leap the inter-religion barrier to become part of today's celebrations. It would be pretty safe to assume that their significance at Hmong New Year is the same as Easter Eggs in the Christian calendar, symbolizing re-birth.

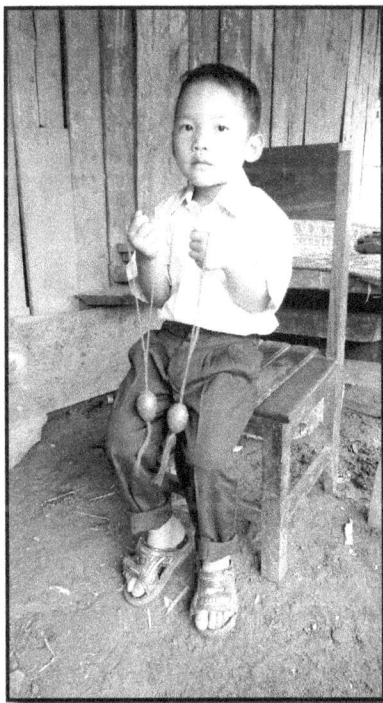

Low and his red eggs

255

Our wrists are already thickly laden with strings and our hearts with blessings when I hear Iain catch his breath as from out of the mêlée and gloom we see Bounyang approaching, slowly, unsteadily, on his walker. His mother, Mi, who appears, without exaggeration, to glow with a Madonna-like beauty, accompanies him.

From the expression on his face we realise Bounyang is absolutely determined to independently tie prayer cords around our wrists. With fierce concentration he finally manages to do so with Iain but by that time he is literally trembling with the exhaustion of the required concentration.

I hold one hand up for him and place the other alongside my face, as I have learnt to do, in a gesture of prayer. With the power of his mind Bounyang forces his uncooperative fingers, to wind the string around my wrist. His mother kneels calmly beside him with an ineffable expression on her face. Slowly, literally painfully slowly, Bounyang ties the knot.

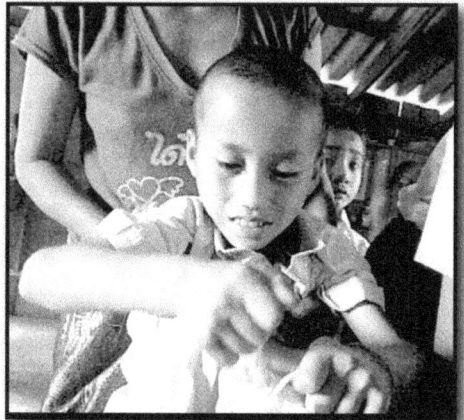

Bounyang tying baci strings on our wrists

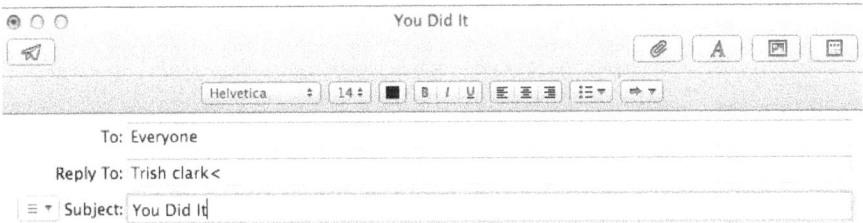

YOU DID IT!

YOU BUILT THE SCHOOL AT PHUJONG!!

CONGRATULATIONS!!! TAKE A BOW...and give the next person you speak to a broad smile and a hug!!!

IT GOES TO SHOW WHAT CAN BE ACHIEVED IF WE ALL WORK TOGETHER!!!!

From this.......

to THIS......

in just on eight weeks.

We wish you were here to share the joy and fun. But we are doing our very best to let everyone in the villages know how happy you are for them.

We have shot a lot of footage and stills and there may

well be a third documentary...and there may even be a follow up to this year's photo-calendars...with one for 2016. I haven't boasted to you yet that they are selling...for full-price...like hot cakes in the UXO (Unexploded Ordnance) Museum in Luang Prabang.

The village of Chillingham...in the caldera of Mt. Wollumbin/Warning on the far north coast of New South Wales...is working towards Sister Friendship with Phoujong/NaLin.

We have collected crayon drawings by the students of Phoujong and NaLin and there are plans for a small exhibition of these alongside drawings by students of the Ethics Class at Chillingham School.

Dearest Ms. Babette has made more beautiful cotton dresses for the girls of the villages.

And all of the uniforms were a special gift from Ged and Denise Brotherton of Brisbane.

COBRA and MONGOOSE (please Google them) an independent aid group established over a decade ago by Michael Symons, who runs a gardening business on Sydney's northern beaches, and who gave $9000 to the Phoujong School Project...has promised an ongoing ANNUAL GIFT OF $500 for the schools at NaLin and Phoujong.

Established on-going financial gifts such as this would be more than welcome (understatement!)...as they would help with forward planning for much needed continuing involvement.

We are hoping to return to Laos in early September for the Official Opening of a School for Phoujong.

We have written a separate HUGE THANK YOU to Pip and Dick Smith...who have made overall donations of $20 thousand in the last four years...importantly these were made at vital times when we could show them nothing and promise them even less. Their trust in us...that demanded nothing in return...was what gave us the courage...some would call it cheek...to start on this undertaking.

We like to think...in truth we know it to be...that the Road to Nalin, Beyond Nalin the Road to Phuong...and now a School for Phuong...will now pass this cheek on and give young children and other villagers a belief in themselves to the extent that they can and will change their lives for the better.

Please stay involved in whatever way you can.

This is not Goodbye...just....

...Sabaidee Pi Mai Lao...Happy New Year...and here comes a huge bucket-load of cleansing water.....

and again Kopchai Lai Lai!

Trish and Iain

14 MAKING BUTTONS

The teak trees are in full bloom; all the way along the Hadsaik River Valley massed cream-coloured flowers top these huge tropical trees like a heavy mattress that stretches to the distant horizon. Their density appears to create a second cloud cover beneath the very for-real bulging clouds, that themselves brim over with fat, heavy raindrops.

The air is so moist it feels as though with each breath one inhales enough water vapour to fill your lungs and drown. It is as if swimming through air.

The rains have been late this year. Months late. So late crops in the far north of the country have withered and died in the fields. There will be financial woes for many. Now the rains have come, with a vengeance, and there will be terrifying floods and more financial woes for others. Life is harshly unforgiving for so many.

We have spent two days in Luang Prabang trying to pull together the final strands of what was still a very moveable, and to us, unknown feast. Well, to be honest, not we, but them. With one knee having had the chop my other knee is by now giving me so much grief that I am more of a burden than a help so I set myself up at a table in the top floor of Jomo, an air-conditioned café and write lists which I give to Iain and Chanthy.

They disappear into town on another of Chanthy's borrowed motorbikes, thank heavens for generous cousins, and try to fulfil my requests. Every half an hour or so they return with yet another large striped zipped-up plastic holdall. They are drenched. It is too hot to wear plastic rain macs. We all go through what they have tracked down and bought.

Right from the outset I have in mind a minimum of fifty helium-filled brightly coloured and decorated balloons. 'How are we going to transport them from here to Muang Nan?' is Iain's totally rational response. 'On the bus?' he asks. 'And even if we did, how would we get them from Muang Nan to Phoujong?' He looks cross, but I don't feel like being rational. I want this Opening to be a party for the students, not some dull recital of self-aggrandizing speeches by politicians and civil servants.

For a few weeks Chanthy has been trying to nail down the helium balloon seller whom we had seen during the Pi Mai festival in Muang Nan, four months previously and who at the time was transporting a large cloud of these balloons up to Luang Prabang on the roof rack of a taxi-truck. I had noted his mobile number and the ever-willing Chanthy had later tracked him down and got a price: the equivalent of 40cents per balloon. But that balloon seller is now in Sayaboury, in the southwest of the country, though he did give Chanthy the name of another balloon trader in Luang Prabang. This man's price is 50 cents a balloon. 'He is Vietnamese, Chanthy says, before assuring us, 'so he won't bargain.'

'Its not the price,' Iain insists to me. 'Its how we get them there.' He speaks slowly as if to a stubborn child. I nod and look downcast. Iain's patience is legendary. He also knows how much this means to me. So, 'I guess we can ask him if he would come to the School with his helium tank and fill the balloons up there,' he suggests. What a chap!

He and Chanthy have been to the stationery outlet and bought a hundred exercise books with the square lined paper that is used in France and so therefore, as a colonial hangover, also in Laos. There are also a same number of packets of coloured pencils, plus an equal number of lead pencils. Planning ahead they have also purchased Buddhist as well as national flags for use in the exhibition of the pupil's drawings in December at our Sister School in Chillingham. We have brought rolls of double-sided sticky tape as well as large quantities of Blu-Tack with us in our baggage. Be prepared.

Helium balloons tied to taxi-truck

The two of them squelch off into the rain again and a young woman from another table, who must have been eavesdropping, asks to joins me. She is Korean. Since the opening of direct flights from Seoul last year Laos is now awash with Koreans. They are very noticeable. Well-mannered and well dressed. Big strong-looking men and confident-looking women, who often are travelling solo.

Jin-Un, 27, teaches English at High School in Seoul. This is her first time abroad. Yes, she likes Laos, because of the space and the greenery. No, she hasn't been to any of the wats. She supposes she is Buddhist, because 'my Mum is. But I only go to the temple at New Year.' Nor has she been to the museums or even the craft-shops. She has been travelling with a group, of other Koreans of a similar age, and they have 'done' Vientiane and gone tubing on the river in Van Vieng. Now she just wants to visit Luang Prabang's Night Market to buy gifts for family and friends. She came to Laos because she saw a documentary on television about the country. Next year she plans to visit Cambodia. Because she has heard 'it's cool'. Not for the first, or last, time I silently query the value of a tourist industry.

The fellows return with bags full of books from Big Brother Mouse. Written in Lao for all ages of children they are brightly coloured and very appealing. The initial brainchild of former monk, Khamla, the company's slogan is Books That Make Literacy Fun! In an absolute first, their books are all written, designed and published in Laos, a country in which reading for pleasure is still a barely recognised concept. The company started a little over a decade and a half ago, with a tiny room in Luang Prabang that foreigners were encouraged to visit and spend time in reading and chatting informally with local students. It then began producing titles such as *The Cat That Meditated*, based on traditional oral stories passed down through the generations. This was followed by *Bangkok Bob*, *New, Improved Buffalo*, *A Fantastic and Frightening Place* and by a scheme to get these titles and the dozens that have followed out into tiny remote rural communities, like Phoujong and NaLin. The technical and political and even on-the-ground problems and logistics that must have been encountered don't bear thinking about. Now fifteen years later, more than 200,000 Lao children have received their very first book because of Big Brother Mouse and the generosity of supporters from around the world. Look up their website:

Iain has also bought tickets for tomorrow's early morning bus down to Muang Nan. Because of the unwieldy shape, size, weight and nature of our various bags full of things for the villages from the Australian School Road Sign through to seventy children's mounted drawings and now all this additional material, we had toyed with the idea of hiring a four-wheel drive vehicle. But at a cost of $250 we baulked and decided we'd struggle to travel as we always did, by public transport at a cost of fifty kip or US$6 each.

There had been no luck with a tank of helium, but in some small compensation Chanthy knows where to buy cut flowers and realising how disappointed I am by the lack of balloons he promises to buy lots of them, fresh in the morning and somehow get them along to the bus-station.

As a further softener he also promises we will be

able to buy cartons of soy milk, in various flavours and any amount of tooth-destroying sweets, in Muang Nan. I tell him he is a very good and special man and I truly mean it. Nothing is too much or too far for him. He totally gets it and is always prepared to go the extra distance. I am yet again in awe of the workings of the universe that caused our paths to cross.

Iain looks bedraggled and exhausted so we cycle back to our big room at Khoum Xieng Thong, our original home away from home in Luang Prabang, though for this visit there is no Noi, or hospitable Thiem Chanh because they are off visiting family in San Francisco. These would be the brothers and sisters, plus a myriad of cousins, who left at the time of the euphemistically monikered, 'Change of Government'. These people have supported Noi and Thiem Chanh financially through the difficult years of an unstable new form of government, sent funds to help build the guest house and must now, as the quality of life steadily improves in Laos, occasionally wonder if they made the right choice in deciding to emigrate into such an alien and challenging lifestyle. In place of their parents we are hosted by the oldest of their three sons, Chanthaek, whom we have seen grow across five years from an uncertain teenager to a confident young man.

***

The bus is, as always, crammed to capacity, but also as always everyone good-naturedly makes room for everyone else and their possessions of which we have an inordinate amount. The stems of the flowers have been stuck into bricks of that solid sponge material that holds an extraordinary amount of water and is so vital to flower-arrangers worldwide. I find it sometimes bizarre what very poor countries have compared with what they don't have. No double-sided tape or Blu-Tack but plentiful supplies of flower sponge. Our flowers are packed and sealed inside big cardboard boxes and are carefully the last to be stowed in the underneath compartment on top of all the other heavy bags. We have bought croissants and baguettes on our way to the bus station at the early start of what we anticipate will be a very long day. Catnapping however briefly or having what we call a Winston Churchill, is an essential talent on such journeys.

The rain has not ceased throughout the night. The highway is slimy with mud from recent landslips so it is also essential to resign from all thoughts of control.

En route there is a call to Chanthy's mobile from his Father Thongkhanh and I think again how nothing, absolutely nothing, would operate in Laos and most other Least Developed Countries, without access to cheap mobiles and their entire networks. I also wonder again why mobile phones operate throughout the entire, highly mountainous terrain of Laos whereas so much of flat Australia remains inaccessible to mobile coverage. Thongkhanh tells us that the road along the Hadsaik River Valley is, well...its more or less impassable. It has rained heavily all night and only now is the deluge beginning to ease. Headman Dith cannot get out from the village to pick us up but Thongkhanh is trying to find alternative transport. Ten minutes later he is back on line cheerfully informing us that the Department of Education in Muang Nan, the people with whom we signed the contract to build the School, have offered to give it a go.

We might not have been so happy with this turn of events if we had known in advance that the driver of this vehicle was such a ninny.

At this office there is a brief meeting accompanied by the inevitable and very welcome, cup of fragrant Chinese tea, with Messrs. Buanthone and Buanphong who, all those months ago had been the ones to fix the date for this event. This time we discuss how the program of events should occur at the Opening. There is even talk of actual timings which, given the state of the roads and rivers and the usual Lao predilection for fluidity of such things, I think is rather precipitate. It is mentioned that Chanthy will be the translator and that we, which I prefer to think of in the singular as Iain, will be required to speak.

All Iain wants to do at this stage is get on the road with all our gear and get going, so he is not delighted to be reminded that we still need to buy large quantities of flavoured soy milk in small cartons, plus mountains of sweets. But this is done in one of the main street shops where people also smile in welcome. They chat to Chanthy and it is apparent that many of the people in town know why we are back and what is happening.

On the edge of town we wave and smile and call out a Hello to Chanthy's sister-in-law Binh, brother Jai's wife and mother of Sydney. Binh is apparently visiting her mother who runs a shop-house on the edge of town.

'Where's Sydney?' I ask Chanthy?

'He's with Jai in NaLin.' Chanthy pauses slightly before adding, 'He's starting school there tomorrow, rather than in Muang Nan.' Another pause. 'He has family and friends in NaLin so he's happy in the village.'

Ah. So there it is. A slight parental disagreement over which school your child should attend. What parent in Brisbane, Sydney, Melbourne, Hobart, Perth or Darwin has not experienced this agony? And for parents in regional Australia an even more fraught choice. Muang Nan is 'the big smoke' for a kid from NaLin. His Aunt, Bounlee will start teaching at NaLin this school year and can keep an eye all day long on her nephew. Perhaps his Dad wants him to stay a country lad while his mother sees more opportunity in town life. Even in poor Laos there are these choices, with their life-long effects all of which appear so vitally important at the time.

From the moment we leave the few surfaced streets of Muang Nan we are into the thick, slippery mud but it is not this that suddenly forces an Ooh and an Aah from our lips. What is this? We gasp in true amazement.

Because, from the track verge, across the river flood plains, up the slopes and off and away into the hills, even to the distant foot of the mountains there marches in rows, probably without exaggeration, a hundred thousand-plus baby banana trees. We gawp in wonder. When we left last time, four months ago, this massive area, many thousands of hectares at least, was all bare, churned red soil. Where there had been tractors, ploughs, front end loaders, excavators and massive trucks amid the piled wreckage of large, uprooted trees, there is now an established banana plantation on a size and scale that it could only have been brought to realization by one group of people, the Chinese.

We knew from our previous conversations with NaLin Headman Dith that this was what has been planned for the Valley. But hearing and seeing are two very different senses. These then are the trees whose fruit will be transported across Laos's northern border with China and judging by their rapid growth, that could begin to happen as soon as next fruiting season.

Ignorant, uninformed, even biased though it may well be, it is hard, even impossible, not to feel personally aggressed against by such a scene. There is no escaping the instant emotion that the land has been raped. The healthy-looking trees stand in serried rows each with its own strand of black water-tubing; not in use in this the wet season but vital for growth in the hot, dry months that will surely follow. There is not a weed to be seen. The richly green leaves glisten in the recent rain. They emanate a muscular strength and it requires very little imagination to think you can actually hear them grow.

On our return journey, a couple of days later, we discuss our reactions with Stephen Midgely, our friend who is an Australian forestry and agriculture expert. He has worked in these vital areas of the economy for Governments across the entire Asia region for more than forty years and he naturally enough dismisses our 1960s hippy peace/love, Small is Beautiful, reactions as unrealistic. Unrealistic in terms of the present world population; in 1965 there were 3.3 billion people on this planet, in 2015 there are 7.3 billion. By mid this century there will be 9.6 billion and all of them will want their share of while not perhaps the good life then at least a less degrading, just decent life for themselves and their families...and bananas!

Where we naively, even selfishly, see rape and pillage Stephen sees an access to an income that will assist with the terrifyingly difficult climb out of poverty. 'You must see how very badly the people here need help, otherwise you wouldn't be doing what you are doing.' Stephen and his Lao-born wife Dao have themselves built four schools, a bridge, simple housing for eighty people and a beautiful *wat;* all of this in similarly difficult situations to NaLin and

Chinese banana plantation in the Hadsaik River Valley

Phoujong. 'Well this,' he gestures towards the banana trees, 'is what is going to help make that happen.'

In the face of our obvious doubting expressions he adds, 'Think about what the sugar cane has done in the Tweed Valley (our neck of the Australian woods).

I do think about it, often, and try to imagine what our Valley would have look liked a hundred plus years ago before the stands of native forest that crowded along the Tweed River were totally decimated and the river flats planted out with sugar cane. Before the sugar farmers, the cedar getters had already been through and ripped out all those huge, beautiful trees. We live off one of those original cedar-getters roads. I've read the stories written by local people and looked at the photographs and I realise that Tumbulgum Primary School, in our local village, at the turn of the last century was more or less on a par with how Phoujong School is today.

So of course Stephen is correct. But we can't let him off completely. On the side of the track we see several groups of men and women with what are obviously spray pumps and open bags of herbicide and other chemicals. We express our dismay that there appear to be no masks, protective clothing, even gloves. Worse still these villagers are squatting down trackside sharing food from communal bowls of sticky rice, minced raw meat and veggies, with their fingers. The long-term health implications are frightening.

Stephen agrees but reminds us of conditions in Dickensian British factories and coalmines in the early 1800s and how they gradually improved. I have never told him that my Dad suffered all his life from rickets due to malnutrition as a child, or that he began his working life at fourteen down the coal mines of Somerset in the West of England. So he has struck a raw nerve.

We are travelling in a truck and Chanthy, who is yet again squeezed into an impossibly small space between us, tells us that his Mother, Bouchanh, worked in these fields planting banana trees during the months we have been away, in order to save some money for her growing family.

Stephen quizzes him about her wage. It turns out to be the equivalent of US$6.25 a day: more than twice the estimated daily wage across the board in Laos. So here we are pontificating about land use and worrying in our armchair manner about personal rights, when tiny Buachanh is toiling away in the hope of educating her grandchildren, Sydney and Jarrah and putting a bit aside for unavoidable emergencies like sickness and death. Who the hell are we kidding? It is embarrassing.

Stephen continues to get the significant facts and figures from Chanthy and now we are somewhat subdued. Best we just get on with what we are trying to achieve.

'What I would be very happy to see,' Stephen says, 'is that all traditional owners at the very least, have formal surveys, perhaps simply using GPS, to mark their boundaries of their lands.   If no such demarcation takes place, these boundaries will become blurred with time.' I notice that Chanthy, struggling to keep up with Stephen's verbal onslaught, takes this piece of information on board.

There is a slight pause for breath before Stephen turns to me and asks with a sparkle of pleasure in his eyes, 'Have you ever read *The Tropical Agriculturalist*? I think he is trying to give us some mental space by lightening the topic and tone of conversation, so imagining some Graham Green style novel I glibly respond, 'No. But it's a great title.'

'They are an excellent and informative read,' Stephen assures me and I realise the sparkle in his eye is a wee touch of mania and that he is not talking about a book but about a magazine. Of this I am doubly sure when he continues, 'It was a periodical, published irregularly but frequently, at the turn of the last century and in 1986 I unearthed a complete set of them in the Tea Research Institute in the Sri Lankan Highlands. I read every one of them.'

In my mind's eye I conjure up a picture of Stephen stretched out under the fans in the library's humid heat engrossed in scores of yellowing copies of *The Tropical Agriculturalist* and I wonder how his beautiful young wife Dao, they have now been married getting on for fifty years, spent that time. Meantime I still think the magazine title has a certain

Somerset Maughan-ish panache for a novel.

'You should try to get there to read them. They are a great reflection on the times and efforts of some very hard working people when social values were quite different. A very useful historical insight into why some things are as they are today,' I hear Stephen suggest, 'but meanwhile I will email you a very interesting report I read recently on the development of the banana industry by the Chinese in under-developed tropical economies.' And he did.

The Road to NaLin, the one we built, or at least the one we raised the money to build, has stood up well to the depredations of three rainy seasons mostly because of the numerous concrete culverts, which we also put in the following year. The trouble is that our five-kilometre side-road is in so much better condition than the one the Department of Main Roads forged through on the far edge of the village that most of the traffic uses our NaLin Road in order to avoid the deep mud on the Government one. This means that motorbikes and the newly introduced lod-sin all putter and chug past the Sisombuth family home where Bouchanh and Bounlee, with the almost one-year-old Jarrah in her arms, are waiting at the door. Never mind, we must not be selfish.

There have been noticeable changes here too over the past few months. No doubt using some of the monies he earned as Site Supervisor during the building of a School for Phoujong, Thongkhanh has knocked out the back wall of their house and extended the side-walls so as to enclose the squat toilet and slosh-over ablution space within the privacy of their extended family home. This means that outdoor slosh-overs whilst enjoying the moonlight sparkling silver on the rice paddies have become a thing of the past. But it also means that it will be marginally simpler for me with my crook knees to have a wash and brush up, as the floor is not slippery with mould and mud. Or for Bounlee to bathe baby Jarrah. You lose some, you gain some.

Chanthy enjoys some of his Mother's home-cooking while Iain paces the floor...making buttons, we children used to call this when Dad did it...anxious to get up to Phoujong where we plan to put up the display of mounted drawings so as to be ready for tomorrow's ceremony.

To her delight I give Bounlee half of Ms. Babette's second lot of dresses. She will distribute them to some of the girls who missed out last time around. I also give her the pile of beanies I have hand-knitted from all those balls of unused new wool left over from a myriad knitting projects across the years. It is surprisingly cool in the early mornings at the turn of the calendar year and they will get plenty of use. She immediately chooses one for her own son and I enjoy time as a surrogate Nana, dandling Jarrah on my lap and helping him open the box of Lego bricks we have brought for him. He's a quiet, thoughtful baby. Jai arrives with his son Sydney, who has always been far more boisterous than his cousin and to whom we give a set of sturdy tipper trucks and excavators. He immediately sets to with his coterie of cousins and friends to enjoy building a garage from the cardboard and plastic box in which they came. All make that international brmm-brmm noise so beloved of young boys as they enter that magic kingdom of imagination in which no adults exist.

Thongkhanh appears with Uncle Fongsamou and together with an assortment of other men from the village we cram back into the truck and in a vital show of diplomacy we make our first stop NaLin School on the outskirts of the village. Here we are given our first viewing of the new ceilings that were installed in every classroom, using our Project monies, after we had left last time. It is vital, for inter-community harmony that we continue to show as much interest in NaLin as we do in Phoujong. There is not exactly bad blood between the two groups but nor would I say all is peace/love between the Lao Loum of NaLin and the mostly Yao and Hmong people of Phoujong. The situation is such that I am glad Iain and I speak none of these languages because by faking not picking up on the internecine prejudices and low-level antagonisms, though one doesn't need actual language to recognise these, we can be sort of excused for blundering on as we do. I say special hellos to a number of the children who after five years of visits I am beginning to know by name.

NaLin school Principal Phonesith Bounyaphon happily shows us the new ceilings builder Khong and supervisor Thongkhan nailed into place after finishing a School for Phoujong. Through Chanthy he thanks us and tells us how pleased he is that his 130 pupils are no longer daily showered with rotting timbers from ceilings that were put in place five years ago but that have been chewed raw by armies of termites.

Bounlee, who as a teacher is attending the first day of the new school year with baby Jarrah on her back, explains to her superior that we would like the drawings that we are about to put up on the walls at Phoujong to come down to NaLin School for exhibition in six weeks time. Mr. Phonesith beams his approval. And when she elaborates on this by saying that after that they will later all come back to Australia to be exhibited at Chillingham School Mr. Phonesith expresses even more pleasure.

The number of pupils at his school seems to grown exponentially from a lake into a sea even since we have been away. Iain gives out exercise books and pencils and crayons into this ocean of scholars and then invites them all, plus all the staff, to tomorrow's Opening and I realise that the soy drinks and sweets will barely suffice.

Finally we start off on the last and most difficult five or so kilometres of really difficult steep, winding track up to Phoujong. The driver is not a happy bunny. He has managed to negotiate a few slip-slidey patches and even get across a couple of small streams

NaLin School Principal Mr. Phonesith

before NaLin but now, when the going gets really tough, he becomes increasingly anxious and tense. This vehicle is not his own, it belongs to the Education Department and that must be an added stress.

It is no longer raining but cloud hangs in wispy, drenching curtains between the tropical foliage that comes right alongside us hiding whatever terrors certainly lurk therein, while the big rocks on the track throw the vehicle this way and that. There is an anxious silence in the vehicle. No more insouciant chatter.

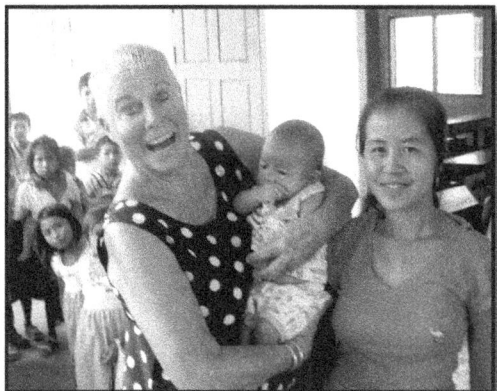

Trish with Jarrah and Bounlee

By the time we reach the stream below the steep uphill lunge that will take us into Phoujong the driver is a mental wreck and the sight of the swift, deep water is the final straw.

While being urged on by all the men he charges at the river, his face strained taut and his heart not in it. He does get across but immediately the wheels hit the mud on the other shore they begin to spin and loose traction. He panics. I try not to, while all the time making plans for how to escape from a hopefully floating vehicle. I find I cannot remember basic lifesaving procedures such as whether you are supposed to keep the windows up or wind them down. I am in the middle of the front bench seat beside the perspiring driver. Iain, who has been sitting beside me for the journey, gets out and joins the rest of the crowd of shouting, pushing men. 'Tell him to let the vehicle run back a small way into the river, then turn the steering-wheel and gun the engine the moment he feels the tyres grip', Iain instructs Chanthy to tell the driver. Wisely Chanthy remains mute. After more shouting of suggestions and wild gesticulating the driver gives it another go and after a very nerve-wracking micro-second in which I feel the truck drift sideways in the rapids I feel the front then the back wheels catch in the mud and churn at first slowly, then with a more steady pace as finally they grasp the earth and travel forward up the steep slope. There is a lot of cheering from the mass of pushing men and I find I need to consciously unclench my jaw.

We don't get far, just a few hundred metres to the first of the village huts. Here the driver adamantly refuses to go further and I agree with his decision. We walk barefoot through the ankle-deep heavy mud the rest of the way, down into a small gully, waving and calling out hellos, before scrabbling up the steep bank to the schoolyard.

We give the building and the toilet block a cursory check and are dismayed to find the ditch that was dug at the back of the School is overflowing with muddy water. Even taking into account that this year's rains are exceptional, it is immediately apparent that we need to have a deep culvert drain, bedded into gravel, installed to remove the danger of the building being undermined, or worse. This can't even be contemplated until the rains stop but while we console ourselves by saying we are glad to have seen the situation at its worst so that we can tell how big the need is, with the immediacy of what needs doing right at this moment we put such plans into our mind's Hold Box and get on with the present.

There is another small panic when we find all the doors are locked but one of my favourite boy students dashes back down through the mud to collect them from the teacher's hut and we are soon all inside enjoying the smell of fresh paint and the sense of security a solid building brings.

Walking barefoot through the mud into Phoujong

Again there is no time for sitting about because already the driver, who seems to have regained his courage, has joined us and is saying that he will not stay long because there is more rain coming, he points to the ominous massed thunderheads, and he needs to get back to Muang Nan before those and nightfall arrive.

We all set to with a will, dragging a couple of big, battered tables into place. On these we lay out the seventy or so drawings face down and Iain gets a production line going. Some helpers use scissors to snip the double-sided tape into small pieces while others tear off bits of Blu-Tack and roll it into smallish balls. Still others place these in each corner of every picture and the rest of the line-up...we have now been joined by people from Phoujong...place the pictures on the walls.

With each one that is displayed, the room becomes increasingly alive, the white walls disappearing under a welter of bright colours. Every one of them is examined, but the ones from Chillingham come under the closest scrutiny. Nothing like this has ever been seen by these people and I find I am looking at 'my culture' as these villagers must be seeing it and finding it extraordinary. Whereas the local ones depict rice paddies, stilt houses, river-fishing and the sun coming up over the mountain; the ones from overseas show large individual houses, big vehicles parked out front, individual bedrooms with television sets and house-pets.

The helpers are especially drawn to the photographs of the pupils from Chillingham holding their own drawings and they pepper Chanthy with questions about them as if he has the answers.

All this time the Education Department driver hangs close by, making buttons and the sky continues to close in. Finally we are finished and we stand back to take everything in at one hit. Spectacular. I just wish all the kids and parents from Chillingham could be here to see the impact. Photographs and footage will not do it justice.

Back down the track we slip and slide in our bare feet to find that the driver has already negotiated the river, which means that we have to walk through, me rather unsteadily, in the knee-deep flow. I am well past bothering to roll up my trouser legs. All I want is to lie down. The driver barely gives us time to all disgorge at the Sisombuth house before he roars off down the track ignoring our parting remarks about looking forward to seeing him when he brings the Education Department dignitaries back up in the morning.

But there is still a baci with close 'family' and friends to be enjoyed and for politeness's sake a meal to be eaten. Neighbour, former Pathet Lao soldier turned carpenter Sengchan wants to discuss the possibility of new desks for which we didn't have enough money last visit and still don't. Headman Dith wants to talk about us assisting with an application from NaLin village to the Australian Embassy's Direct Aid Project for help to build an additional room onto their school during this coming school year. Sydney and his pals are still brmm-brmming their trucks around the floor and there is, as always, talk of rice crops, pigs and the weather.

285

Chanthy pinning up the drawings in Phoujong

At some time mid-evening I gorge my painkiller pills, unroll my thin kapok mattress onto the tile floor and pass out. I don't hear people leave nor sense the lights going off but when I wake in the early hours of the following morning I realise I am still lying in exactly the same prone position, as I was when I fell into a stupor.

15 THE DAY ARRIVES

Of course it is not possible for a man to grow fifteen centimetres in a single day.

Or is it?

Could it be there is magic abroad in Phoujong on September 1st 2015 because that is certainly what seems to happen to sole teacher Kaojien Zaethan who for eleven long years has been asking the Education Department for a new schoolhouse and has not even been given the courtesy of a reply. He starts this day as a regular guy, though certainly one with a warm personality. But by the end of it I swear he has physically stretched to the extent that he stands that much taller, smiles more broadly and looks everyone in the eye with a 'Yep I'm your man and this is my place,' look on his face.

The mobile phone calls begin before dawn. Iain and I, pretending to ourselves and to each other that we are still asleep, can hear the calm tones of Thongkhanh. What a great top executive of a major multi-national company or political leader he would make! Ready for whatever unexpected demands are dumped in his lap while also ready to delegate.

Sounding very low 'Did you hear the rain?' Iain asks into the darkness. 'It didn't let up all night.' I have to admit that I didn't, but try to leaven my seeming callousness by suggesting it was the deadening drugs that blocked my ears. 'I can't see how we can possibly get back up to Phoujong this morning,' Iain sounds miserable. Five decades of intimacy have taught me that no bland generalities will help. What he needs is to get up and have a shave, a shower and a hot drink.

Buachanh pads down the stairs and crosses to the kitchen from where we can hear her lighting the fire and putting the day's rice on to heat through. I roll out from under the mosquito net that someone must have kindly suspended over us. Iain does the same and while I begin, painfully slowly, to let down the net and fold back the thin kapok mattress he goes off for a slosh-over. By the time he returns looking, in the already increasing light, a great deal happier, Chanthy is stirring under his net and I gimp off to get my own turn at the water tub and squat loo.

When I come back, everyone is up and Thongkhanh and Iain are full of the bright news that although the driver from the Education Department has called to say he won't be able to get through Thongkhanh has already tracked down the driver of a hugely sturdy four wheel drive truck who is game enough to attempt the journey from NaLin up to Phoujong.

Over a breakfast of sticky rice and some minced material of unknown provenance, plus eggs that, yet again, Chanthy has managed to purchase somewhere in the village, we discover that the driver, Mr.Chanmany, works for Vieng Vone, a large construction company presently employed in southern Laos to construct yet another hydro-electric dam. He is making a short visit to his wife and children in Phoujong and is more than happy to help out by making the difficult journey down from there, to pick us all up and drive us back up the same strenuously demanding route. Serendipity strikes yet again.

'It's a pity about the Education Department people not being able to come,' I say to Iain, trying to commiserate. 'They'll come,' he states, with the look I have seen so many times before that I know better than to make any further comment.

Before the day's proceedings totally swallow us up we are determined to catch up with Thongdy Thongsamou, the man who is even older than Iain! the

289

village *morphon* or master of blessings whose wife, though much younger than him, had died unexpectedly just before we left last time. Following her death Thongdy has lost any will to live and when we had said goodbye then we had neither of us expected to see him alive again. When we asked around among people of the village they all tell us that he no longer works his rice-fields or spends time with others outside his immediate family, instead preferring to see out his days sitting on the tiny balcony of his house, staring into space.

I have chosen to wear the simple handmade blessing string and metal necklace he had given me some years previously in the hope this will be a conversation opener. I also have a special woolen beanie I knitted for him because I had seen him so many times leaving the village at first light to go to his fields with an ancient, unraveling beanie on his head to keep out the early morning chill.

Chanthy goes up the rickety stairs and softly calls, 'Thongdy. Thongdy. Iain and Trish are here from Australia.' There is a longish wait and then dear Thongdy shuffles out, heartbreakingly disheveled and bleary-eyed. He comes slowly down the stairs and we all hug. He is, if possible, thinner than ever, a faded shadow of his former self, so obviously wanting the last of life's little day to ebb away. His voice reduced to a wan whisper he holds our hands and tells us, again, his wife has died and he wants to join her.

Chanthy tells him that today we are opening a School for Phoujong and I like to think his eyes brightened. But that's just an ego-driven self indulgence on my part. We have shared so many jokes, mostly about his and Iain's great ages and he has officiated at so many of the baci, or soul-strengthening, occasions we have been a part of in the village. But it is time for him to leave this world if only because he wants to. I place the beanie gently on his head of wispy hair. He hugs us farewell though as he does so he touches our necklace and gives the tiniest of smiles. Travel well Thongdy.

Thongkhanh arrives to let us know our transport to Phoujong has come. We walk back up to the Sisombuth home and are somewhat surprised when we meet the truck driver, Mr. Chanmany. He looks so like a cartoon version of an American oil-rig, or mine worker in his good working gear topped by a cap whose brim is emblazoned with V.V., the initials of his company, that I fully expect him to proffer his hand to shake while inquiring 'How y'all doing? But of course he doesn't. Instead he *nops* and gives a slow smile before politely helping me into the cabin of his truck that wouldn't be out of place in one of those wild giant 4-wheel drive derbies so beloved by a certain sector of the male population in North America and Australia. He looks very at home and comfortably in charge behind the wheel of this heavy-duty vehicle, exuding so much confidence that its excess spreads across us all, filling us with the belief that we'll easily master this journey with energy to spare.

The rain has stopped chucking it down but it still fills the air with a lung clogging threat as Chanmany throws his truck, loaded with villagers, into gear and aims it at the track. He is an immensely skillful driver, at one with his vehicle and the way ahead. Going at a steady, determined rate he never pauses even at the final hurdle, the stream at the entrance to the village that has developed overnight into deeper, faster, rapids We are through the swirling water and up into the village itself all in one smooth move. When I thank Chanmany with heart-felt expressions of relief as I clamber out into the mud he accepts my praise of his skills with a smile of acknowledgement.

Once again we struggle barefoot through the clogging mud down into the small gully and up the slope on the other side into the school grounds that are already alive with people. A large tub of water has been placed at the far end of the verandah and we take turns to stand in it and wash off as much of the surplus mud as possible. This has quickly become so engrained in our feet, especially between the toes, that in spite of vigorous scrubbing the flesh remains stubbornly mud-hued for a couple of days.

The students, smart in the new school uniforms we

gave them four months before and had obviously not been worn during the summer break, but instead saved for this occasion, are already seated in rows on woven matting in the classroom, whose walls are now so bright with their drawings. They look excited and expectant. Kaojien in his smart khaki teacher's uniform welcomes us. I am aware of being over-excited and only just manage to control my urge to hug him. Instead, as a poor second-best, we all *nop* each other madly and grin broadly.

From this moment on time appears to become elastic, sometimes stretched to breaking point, while we wait anxiously for others to arrive, sometimes whizzing by with such speed and so chockablock with many happenings and people that I feel giddy and out of my body.

The long tables that were so useful yesterday are again called into action and we begin to unwrap our parcels as the children watch carefully. Someone produces a very large battered, aluminium cake-stand/ baci platter on which we display some of the small cartons of flavoured soymilk. There is a murmur of anticipation as we shake out piles of sweets. The bright flowers, that mercifully have survived intact, also draw appreciative whispers. I have a moment of sadness that I haven't managed the helium balloons.

A huge handmade sign, in Lao script, has been hung

on the wall at one end of the room and other tables have been placed beneath this. I can only assume it is an announcement of the Opening.

There is a smell of cooking food and for the first time I notice the scores of women who are clustered around open fires under the attap thatch roof of the lean-to attached to the old shack of a schoolhouse. This building is still standing. Just. Of course the villagers are not going to take it down. To make room for what? Sculptured gardens and playing fields? I don't think so. How wrong can one be? Anyway, right now its adjacent lean-to is being utilized as a cookhouse.

From across a sea of mud I recognize some of the women while others I have never seen before. I wave and they wave back before continuing to chop and mince, fry and grill. Two large pigs have been slaughtered for the feast to come...and a buffalo. How the women got both themselves and the produce and meat here and when, I have no idea and I never find out, like so much else that happens on this day.

The sun miraculously breaks through so that now steam rises from the mud that begins to get a fine crust on it. I see Iain in a huddle with Chanthy and his Father, Thongkhanh. They all seem to be on their phones talking at the same time. Then suddenly Thongkhanh is no more and Chanthy and Iain are beside me with Iain informing me that the Education Department driver has been shamed into bringing his passengers as far as NaLin. But he is adamantly refusing to go any further.

Iain has hardly finished imparting this information, with a degree of irritation, when his phone rings again. It is Ms. Jodie and Ms. Mouth from the Australian Embassy in Vientiane. Jodie Rogers is Consul and Second Secretary. Sayasith Phongsamouth is the senior Lao official for the Embassy's Direct Aid Program, who okay-ed the $10,000 grant to the Project.

The two women have flown up on the previous day to overnight in Luang Prabang. Iain has been in communication with them and suggested they buy wellington boots at the Chinese market. Now it seems that they are on the road from LPB, being driven in a hired four-wheel drive vehicle, crammed to overflowing with large cardboard boxes containing extra new school uniforms for both Phoujong and Nalin schools. He tells them about the state of the track in and they discuss the possibility that by the time they get to Muang Nan, if there is no more rain, they will give it a go.

If they get then get as far as NaLin perhaps they can give a lift to the two stranded Education Department officials? Usually we wouldn't be worried about missing out on the company of these two local civil servants. But today is far from usual. These men represent far more than the Education Department, though that would be enough reason to want them here. They represent, at one remove, the Government of Laos.

So come what may...they HAVE to attend: if only to be the face, not only of the Education Department, but the Government at large. The people of Phoujong could not care less if they come or not. If they don't it will simply be another example of the expected lack of care by the Government. So, they must come. Iain is determined.

Chanthy and I exchange brief glances. This young man has had us worked out for years. He recognizes our moods. So he knows better than to give voice to any suggestions or comments. He is his Father's son. Or perhaps just Buddhist.

Iain's mobile sings again. This time its Stephen. Of Stephen and Dao. The man with faith that a squillion bananas offer a better future and who reads *The Tropical Agriculturalist* in his spare time. Dear Stephen and Dao they have been such an on-the-ground comfort and support to us over this half-decade and now they are stuck deep in the mud on the track through those self-same fruiting trees. But never fear, Stephen has seen his way out of many worse situations than this and they will certainly reach us. Right at this moment the equally formidable and determined Dao is chatting up the Chinese manager of a group of men working on the aforementioned banana plantation who just happened on them, stuck up to their axle on the track, another piece of serendipity. With the blessing of her impeccable Chinese conversation skills she is addressing him as 'Honorable Mr. Boss-man' and asking for his help. Dao is a very attractive woman and Mr. Boss-man, soon won over, is at this very

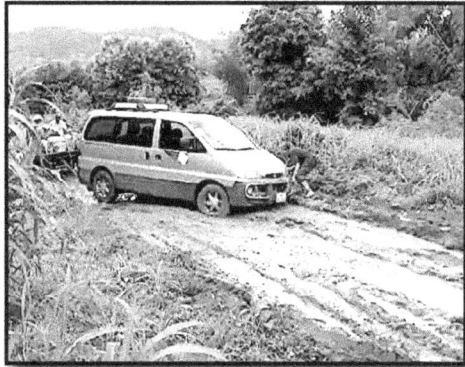

Dao and Stephen's vehicle stuck in the mud

moment attaching his muscular lod-sin to their vehicle and pulling them to the far side of the bog.

'We'll be with you shortly,' Stephen shouts with enthusiasm down the phone and isn't even fazed when Iain asks him if they would mind making a one-kilometer detour via our road through NaLin in order to pick up the stranded Education Department blokes, just in case Mouth and Jodie don't make it.

Iain then has a one-sided conversation, via Chanthy, with these men from Education Department to inform them that rescue is on the way and that they WILL be attending the opening of a School for Phoujong. He sounds triumphant.

Thongkhanh is back, perhaps by motorbike perhaps by magician's broomstick and with him he has Mr.

Khong the builder of the school. Through Chanthy, we had invited Mr. Khong to come to the Opening armed with a battery powered electric drill. Obviously he doesn't have one because when we show him the Australian School Sign we want put up he produces a few nails and a hammer and moves to bash holes in the wall. Sacrilege! The sign is to have its home on the wall above the sidesteps up to the Principal's office. Speaking of whom, Kaojien has materialized from out of the growing crowd and it is now that I notice for the first time his increase in height; perhaps just three centimetres. He takes the sign and places it just so, this is where he wants the sign attached: his school, his decision. Six centimetres.

Several nails are used in order to gradually make the necessary holes deep enough. Magician Thongkhanh produces a small packet of rawlplugs, Mr. Khong hammers these into the nail-holes and placing the sign, just as directed, he uses a much-abused screwdriver to attach the sign to the wall. We all stand back to admire the effect. Splendid.

Khong puts up the school sign

I decide that, with everyone from the various official parties now seemingly on the way, its time for me to spiff myself up a bit, well at least as far as such a thing is possible under these conditions.

Taking my bag with me I try tiptoeing across the mud to the toilet block; three individual squat loos over which so much time and heartache has been extended. Two of them are locked, seemingly from the outside. The third has a large bunch of freshly cut banana leaves propped inside against the wall, making it impossible to shut the door. Ah well, the Lao are well-known for their politeness and discretion so who is going to bother to peek at an elderly woman changing her clothes, but still I do try to be as quick and discreet as I can, while balancing precariously on my leg with a dodgy knee.

I slip on the dress I have had tailored by Yvonne at the Gold Coast. It is made from a beautiful piece of hand-embroidered material given to me by Chanthy just as we left Lung Prabang after the building of the School. In yet another example of his caring he has picked up on my appreciation of indigenous handicrafts and chosen a piece of intricate work from Xiengthong Province. I love it but it is delicate and has to be carefully sewn into a lined dress that shows off its individualistic qualities. Yvonne has done a great job and as I put it on, together in a few minutes, with a pair of decent, though necessarily flat, red shoes and being a mere woman, I am immediately lifted above the heat and mud!

Iain and Trish with the Children's Drawings

I cross back onto the verandah and walk into Iain who has coincidentally but with great perspicacity also changed into a pair of good shoes and trousers plus a traditional style Lao shirt, another thoughtful gift from Chanthy. Together, my sister would say if she was here, we look like a pair of faded matinee idols. But I tell you what, the Phoujongers appreciate our act of respect and there are smiles all around.

Then it is back to the business at hand as we hear the loud chug-chug-chug of a lod-sin working its way up the slope bearing Dao and Stephen, plus Bounthone Sithidphone, from the Education Department. He is without his sidekick, who perhaps is too nervous to attempt the trip. But *bo peng yang*, one is better than none and Bounthone, although not wearing his Department's military-style khaki uniform, will be a sufficiency to show Government cares.

Dao springs from the vehicle, all bright smiles, wearing as always the style of clothing any other Lao woman would only dare to wear in her dreams; bright coloured bottom-hugging cotton trousers shown off to perfection by a neat well-cut white blouse. She greets everyone as if she has known them for years and after the initial surprise, not to say shock, everyone wants to meet the fascinating woman who though she is obviously Lao slips with smooth

Dao & Stephen arrive at Phoujong

confidence, great warmth and style from language to language, culture to culture making no missteps. There is not a person in Phoujong or NaLin who would have met such a creature before.

By contrast husband, Stephen comes a very poor second, even with his Lao language skills. Everybody wants to meet them both but Lao manners demand this happens slowly. 'We left our vehicle on the other side of the rapids outside the village and then hitched a ride with this lod-sin', Stephen tells us before going on to recount the full story of the fortuitous meeting with the Chinese manager of the banana plantation work-team.

Bounchanh, Dao's longest-standing female Lao friend, who attended her marriage in Vientiane in the midst of the Change of Government in 1975, accompanies them. Also Bounchanh's own husband Pheng. There must be a massive back-story to this decades long friendship but one we have yet to fully uncover.

A happy Kaojien shows them all the School Sign, another five centimetres maybe, who then takes them on a guided tour of 'his school.' Definitely a further four!

Bounthone, the Education Department chap, barely gets any attention so he feigns a lingering interest in the sign and as I am standing language-useless alongside him I notice a man I have never seen before. He appears to be translating the Lao language part of the sign for others who crowd around. This man has enviably smooth ageless skin and a rather tight expression. I surreptitiously check the bottom of his wide-legged black trousers. Yes, there it is, the telltale fine hand-stitched red hemline. So though he could possible be Hmong, in this village he is more than likely to be Yao. He is running his manicured nail, a most unusual sight in Phoujong, underneath each line of the Lao writing and retelling it, in what is to my admittedly cloth ears, Chinese.

I rush to get the folder of plastic sleeves in which I carry various, to me at least, important documents. I return to show this man, who has not come across our radar before, probably because we are mere *falang,* the enlarged photograph I had previously taken of the calligraphy on the outside wall of Teacher Kaojien's house.

When we went back to Australia last time I had shown the enlargement to our local chemist, Nelson

Louie, who is Hong Kong Chinese. He and his wife, Judy, also Hong Kong Chinese, happily translated the calligraphy as a complex date with many sidebars of information. Judy assured me that though 'the calligraphy is excellent, the work of an educated person, the grammar is 'not so good.'

Through Chanthy I explain to this man, who I am beginning to realize, from the attention being given to him by other villagers, is a Big Man in the community, that I had the translation done and what Judy had said, leaving out the comment about the poor grammar of course. I do this to show him I am interested. His response is a complete lack of interest.

I ask him if he is Yao and he looks at me as if I am a mere outsider and nods peremptorily. Then I ask if he is translating the Lao words on the sign into Yao. I get another dismissive nod. I manage to ask how long he has lived in the village and I get the abrupt advice that he has been here since the Government moved it down from the mountains, seventeen years previously.

So, here's the man I have wanted to meet: the keeper of the village history, traditions and language. I curse myself for not having found him previously. From the start of the idea for the School Sign I had wanted it to be written in three languages.   Lao, the national language; English, the mother tongue of most of the donors and Yao, the language of the villagers.

Everyone knows language is vital to the on-going strength and health of a culture. Australians know it even more than most because so many Aboriginal languages have died from willful neglect. Through Chanthy I had asked Kaojien, who denied knowing what the calligraphy on his wall meant, if he knew of someone who could write Yao. I had asked Headman Laisiew. I had even eaten enough humble pie to ask Scowler Sinfan. All responses were negative. The door was quite blatantly shut in my face in much the same way and for the same reasons as Aboriginal people deny knowledge to white Australians.

I had driven Iain almost crazy with stories of how when I was growing up in England in the 1950s the Welsh language, spoken in homes just across the River Severn from my own county, was banned in schools and came dangerously close to being lost. But some brave souls kept in the face of the authorities and today Welsh is back as a living language in Cyrmu; still struggling, yes, because the deadening hand of the Thames Valley bureaucrat is everywhere, but managing to hang in there.

Yes, I get it that tribalism may often be a curse in the modern world, but on the other side of the coin, as so often, it is surely the blessing of self-respect.

So here's the man, I am now more than sure he is the village shaman, who could have helped with the Yao translation of the sign but who, for whatever reasons, declined. He was here, in the shadows all the time. I am disappointed. Is it too much to imagine that he senses this? As I go to close my folder he reaches out to one of the pages, the one that shows the photograph Iain took of the X-ray of my brand new knee. I had brought it to show friends in NaLin, in particular Headman Dith who had been so amused by the idea of a replacement metal knee. This Yao man, I never find out his name, and he disappears as smoothly and completely as he appeared, takes the file from my hands and studies what of course to him is an extraordinary piece of technology. I show him the long scar on the front of my knee. He queries Chanthy who by now is almost as familiar with the intricacies of what is involved in total knee replacements as I am myself. The man studies it with all the interest that I had shown in his language and in the weeks that follow, since when I've had time to digest and make some sense of everything that had happened on that special day, I wonder if there isn't some deeper correlation between language and invasive surgery. Something I am still mulling over.

There is no time in this present for such thinking because another lod-sin battles its noisy way up the hill. Perched right on the front is Ms. Mouth and Ms. Jody, both wearing black, shiny obviously new, wellington boots. They have been picked up from the other side of the rapids at the edge of the village, where they have left their vehicle and are both smiling with the joy of it all.

Australian Consul
Jody Rodgers
arrives with
Sayasith
Phongsamouth

Chugging up close behind is another lod-sin, the one all the men have been waiting for because piled high on both ends are the familiar bright yellow-coloured crates of Beer Lao.

As scores of willing men begin to happily offload the crates of amber fluid, two huge cardboard boxes are revealed which we presume hold the school uniforms, the additional generous donation from the Australian Embassy. These boxes are carried in to the classroom and seem to signal that the official proceedings can now get underway.

Somehow or other Iain and I find ourselves walking along the verandah of the long-dreamt of School for Phoujong between rows of clapping uniformed students, being presented with bouquets of flowers, all of which I realise must have been organized by Dao, and led to seats behind the long table. Mouth and Jody join us. Seated at a side table are the Education

Department's Bounthone and most importantly Teacher Kaojien Zaethan, plus ten centimetres! Rows of children, their eyes bright with expectation, smile up at us from the floor mats. It is only now I see how many of them there are and realise that large numbers of pupils from NaLin have walked their way up along five kilometres of muddy, rocky track to join in the fun. All those open hearts. All that potential. All that need.

Fortunately the speeches were over quickly, though I like to think everyone who needed to had their moment in the sun. Chanthy, the lynchpin, kept up with the forwards/backwards translation demands.

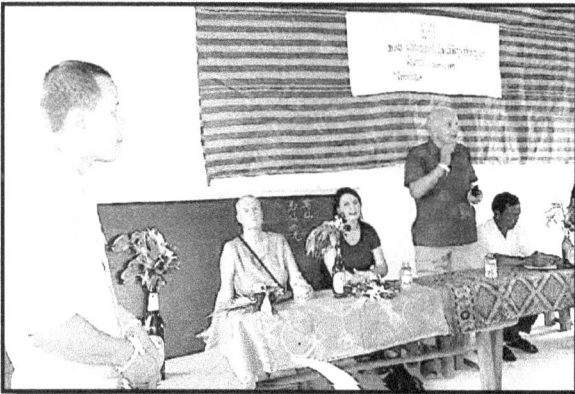

Chanthy translating Iain's exceedingly brief 'speech' at the opening.

Suddenly the formalities were complete and the children were rewarded for their exceptional patience.

Ms. Mouth and Ms. Jodie ripped open the cardboard boxes and with no attempt at trying to give out the correct sizes, 'they'll work all that out among themselves,' Mouth assured us, she and Jodie piled a *sin* or trousers plus shirts into the outstretched arms. Chanthy and I, leaving Iain free to capture something of the madness on film, added exercise books, crayons, pencils, a carton of flavoured soy milk and finally a handful of sweets, on top and each child staggered happily away with their horde. At some point I realize some of them, the boys of course, were coming around for a second time. But so what. Good on them I say. Also at some point I realize that crippled Bounyang is on the floor, having given up on the possibility of manouvering his walker through the throng, waiting patiently to be noticed and I bend down to load up his distressingly thin arms.

The table has barely been cleared of its goodies than we are ushered into the adjoining classroom where mats have again been spread on the floor and a lovingly handmade *phakhoun*, or altar of flowers, sits on a special platter in the middle, adorned with sticks of blessing strings. The body of a plucked and boiled chicken is curled around the base.

Dearest Thongdy, how much we miss him, but Uncle Fonsamou fills in as *morphon* with grace even managing to make a small joke about this being the first occasion on which he has taken on this role. The spirits are called in. Strings tied on wrists. Blessings given. As always I think how impossible it would be to hold on to petty jealousies and resentments while sharing in such an occasion.

Someone or thing must have been the organisational mover and shaker behind the day because now we find that in the other classroom the floor mats have been removed and the tables formed up with, thank heavens, benches. Food is being brought over in prodigious quantities from the women's cooking place, though of course there are no women, other than Dao and me, sitting at the tables. The beer is beginning to flow in copious amounts.

But before we can answer insistent calls for us to come join in Chanthy appears with Xienguanh, Buanyang's Father, alongside him. Before we understand what is happening Xienguanh is pressing three thousand kip, less than 50 cents, into Iain's hand. Iain attempts to give it back but Xienguanh steadfastly refuses. We catch the eye of Chanthy, who as always knows what should be done and I take the money from Iain's hand, put it behind my back, thank Xienguanh and then bringing the notes out in the other hand, place them gently back with Xienguanh.

We fully understand that he wants to thank us for being of small assistance to his crippled son, but we also know that three thousand kip is much more to him than it is to us.

I am sorely tempted to let this burdened father

know that a wonderful new walker will be coming for Bounyang in a couple of month's time

He is a special lad. You can see such intelligence in his eyes that you know how much he would blossom with additional help. We have met a young man who like Bounyang has also been half-crippled with polio since birth and who has been greatly assisted by Dao and Stephen and their Canberra supporters. He has completed his education and is now establishing, of all things, a frog farm business. So, with the help of others, more can and will be done for Bounyang.

Ms. Mouth and Ms. Jodie have decided that staying for the feast might also include, due to inclement weather, an uncomfortable overnight stay on the floor of a hut and they have a flight to catch. So they have decided not to push their luck further and leave while the going is good. We wave them goodbye with many thank yous. Later we learn that Ms. Mouth, who is a daughter of one of those well-to-do families who are so influential in the running of the country, had never before visited a village such as Phoujong. So its not only us *falang* who are learning big lessons from all of this.

On the way back to the food table I get a brief glimpse of goings on in the Principal's room. A table is set up here too and four very attractive young women are seated, interspersed, between Phoujong Headman Laisiew, NaLin Headman Dith and the Education

Department chap Bounthone. They are ploughing into plates of food, quaffing bottles of beer and the atmosphere is extremely convivial.

They all look rather embarrassed at my appearance so I very quickly withdraw. Same, same, but different, all around the world. The perks of power.

There is a similar conviviality in the main schoolroom. I squeeze in on one of the benches next to Sanfin, making unintelligible, to him, remarks of bonhomie but hoping he will pick up on my positive tone of voice. This is not the day to be making ungracious remarks about his unhelpfulness. Though I later learn that he put the hard word on Dao, sitting opposite us, for some financial help from them for his village. Fair enough, being in his situation I might well have done the same, though of course Dao told him that he should approach Iain and Trish for any further assistance.

On the far side of the room I can see Teacher Kaojien in animated conversation with everyone around him. He beams me a smile. Fifteen centimetres taller at least because he is no longer simply Teacher Kaojien, he is Principal Kaojien having been informed that as he now has two classrooms the Education Department has assigned him a junior teacher who will take classes in the second room. Of course they both know there may well still be several months between pay packets, that's almost to be expected. But it suddenly dawns on me that the idea mooted by architect Justin Twohill all those months ago at the beginning of the year when he had suggested that we should think of The School, see how it always deserves capitals!, as more than a School but as a Community Centre for the whole village has actually materialised. At the time we had more or less dismissed the idea, or at least the nomenclature, on the grounds that Community Centres are an idea too far in remote villages and that all get-togethers in Phoujong had up to now occurred in the dimness of electricity-less individual huts. But look around you; here it is, happening for the very first time, a village celebration, happening in a solid building, in Principal Kaojien's more than a School for Phoujong.

I am far too excited to eat the minced raw pork, though I do manage some mouthfuls of water spinach. Photographs of the students at Chillingham beam down at us from the walls. I wish they were all here. I wish all our supporters were here too. By showing unmerited belief in us they deserve to share the joy.

What a day this has been.

16 A WRAP

So that's a wrap.

Well of course it isn't quite that because this isn't a television shoot its real life and the Phoujong School Project has taken on an unexpected and heart-warming life of its own.

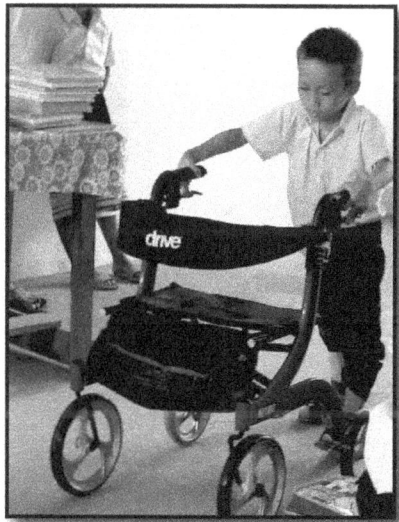

Bounyang test drive

A few months after we came home, Julie West, who taught Iain some of his movie-making techniques at our local TAFE, went on her second visit to Phoujong to take a top-of-the-line walking aid, that she had provided herself, up to eight-year-old Bounyang. Julie is returning to Laos again and plans to talk through with Bounyang's parents her proposed new offer to sponsor him through a full education. Words are not sufficient.

Using the drawings by students at Phoujong and NaLin, that Julie brought back and mounting them together with the drawings by Chillingham pupils, we held an exhibition at Chillingham School that then went on to be displayed at the village Community Centre, whose monthly markets get big numbers of visitors from not only the caldera area of the beautiful Mt. Wollumbin but from much further afield.

Through more good work by Ethics Teacher Neville Jennings, the sistering of these schools has been extended into a tripartite scheme to now include students at the primary school in the Aboriginal lands of Elcho Island in Australia's Northern Territory.

Anita from Elcho Island

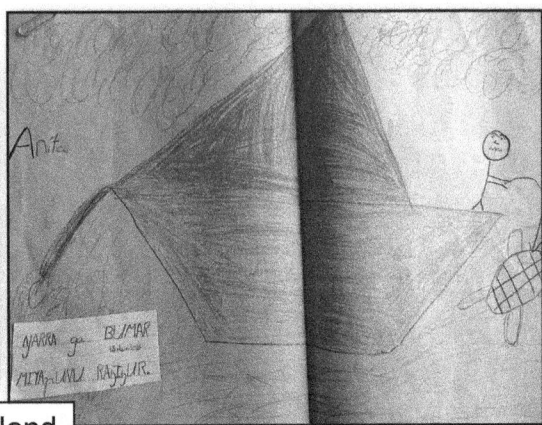

Explaining Elcho and her people to the kids in Phoujong and NaLin as well as enlarging Elcho Island kid's knowledge of Laos is exactly the hands-on, ground-level communication we are keen to develop.

314

In addition, Meg Ayers at Lindisfarne, a local private school here in the Tweed, has suggested they would like to take their Year Eleven students on an active visit as part of her Pastoral Care Programme and the Australian Embassy in Vientiane have offered to be involved with that.

In yet another good development, Doctor Ed Egan, an Emergency Doctor at Tweed and Murwillumbah Hospitals, after reading my book *The Road to NaLin*, is going up to Luang Prabang later this year and has volunteered his desperately needed professional services at the Lao Friends Hospital for Children. This is a brand new facility and one of three hospitals built in Cambodia and Laos by the internationally acclaimed Japanese phtographer Kenro Izu. Doctor Ed will be accompanied by his Croatian born wife Kathy and their two Primary School-aged children.

During the year it has taken to get Iain's documentary and this book finished several other friends have been welcomed on visits to the villages and their follow-up enthusiastic emails complete with photographs show how much the children have been affected for the good by all these happenings. They are more self-assured, confident even, in the low-key Laos manner.

Principal Kaojien is running his new school, with the assistance of the new teacher, with verve and imagination. The walls are decorated with children's drawings and he even has a botanical display, in glass jars, on a work-bench.

Building material from the old school shack has been rescued and used to build a smaller attached classroom for the youngest students.

For us this is a big example of what people can and will achieve when simply given the opportunity. We always sensed that Kaojien was out of the box and all of this confirms that.

It also means the students have made the first step in understanding the concept of there being a bigger world, outside of Laos, where people know about them and care for their well-being. All this adds up to a development of vital self-respect.

The villagers have taken ownership of the new building by clearing a super-sized open space in front of the school and erecting a very strong, pig-proof surrounding wooden fence.

We, of course, plan to continue our involvement with Phoujong and NaLin villages, with the school now the main focus, but we have decided this has to be our last filmic and writing adventure in Laos. Better to focus our energies on cosseting along what has been achieved.

We want to make a tentative foray into the world of computer literacy with the older students. So we are looking for a way to entice some electronics firm like JB Hi-Fi or Harvey Norman to help in some way with computers or tablets.

We would also like an intensive short-course teacher-training-programme to be held to upgrade the skills of the very poorly supported local teachers. There's an on-going need for writing materials and Lao language reading books and there will always be building maintenance required, because Laos has a very damaging tropical climate.

From out of left field there is also the concept of establishing best practice pig farming. For this we are getting a helping hand from ACIAR, the Australian Centre of International Agricultural Research, based in Canberra.

We now have a handful of annual sponsors and in the latest good news two of these, professional gardener Penny Hunstead and her astrophysicist husband Richard, who is revered enough to have a comet named after him, have taken on financial responsibility for NaLin Headman, Mr. Dith's daughter Nit to undergo her three year nursing training.

This regular Annual Sponsorship idea is something we want very much to grow and encourage. It would relieve some of the constant uncertainty that is something like living hand to mouth ourselves and also help us to set long-term goals.

None of this had been planned in advance. But it has all somehow grown into existence organically.

Sometimes it is difficult to believe it is happening. It is almost as though we have tapped into a well of goodwill. It certainly brings out the best in many people both here and there. It brings happiness. And you can't hope for more than that.

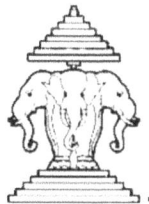

LAO WORDS

Wat	Place of worship
Naiban	Village Headman
Falang	Foreigner
Nop	Polite form of greeting. (Hands raised to forehead palms together)
Attap	Not Lao word. Used inMalaysia. (Palm leaves sewn together to form roofing material)
Laap	Minced and chopped meat or fish. A staple Lao food.
Bo peng yang	No worries.
Sabaidee	Hello. Goodbye.
Baci	Animist religious ceremony. (Calling in the 33 kwan, or pieces of one's soul)
Pho	Soup
Pho pak	Vegetable soup
Lao Loum	Majority people of Laos
Yao	Minority people of Laos
Khmu	Minority people of Laos
Hmong	Minority people of Laos
Kopchai	Thank you
Kopchai lai lai	Thank you very much
Tuk tuk	Vehicle carrying multiple passengers (taxi)
Tok tok	Heavy-duty rural truck-like vehicle
Lodsin	Chinese replacement for tok tok
Lao-lao	Lao rice whisky
Morphon	Spirit man
Stupa	Resting place for human remains
Sin	Wraparound skirt for females
Apsara	Angel
Pi Mai	New Year
Phakhoum	Central prayer tree for baci

ABOUT THE AUTHOR

Trish Clark has been a journalist all her working life, a period of over fifty years, in which she has worked as a newspaper columnist, a feature writer for major magazines and newspapers, a radio broadcaster and television reporter, as well as a producer of radio and television programs that have been broadcast nationally and internationally.

She helped establish and worked with the internationally successful science program for television, *Beyond 2000*, which was aired by the Discovery Channel for more than a decade.

In 2003/4 Trish spent 18 months working, with her husband, Iain Finlay on the Voice of Viet Nam Radio network, as Editors and Radio Programmers, while training local Vietnamese reporters in English usage, editing and on-air presentation techniques.

Since 2011, she and Iain have been involved in three major projects they developed together in two remote villages in northern Laos. First, building a decent road to the vilage of NaLin, then a series of 16 large culvert drains over a distance of some ten kilometres to NaLin and Phoujong villages. And most recently in 2015...and the subject of this book, building a new primary school for the village of Phoujong

Trish is the author of eleven books, which include a biography, as well as fiction and non-fiction publications, five written jointly with Iain, on Africa, South America and the South Pacific, Viet Nam and Central Asia. She and Iain have children and grandchildren and when not traveling, live in Australia in the Tweed Valley, in northern New South Wales.

Read about other titles by Trish Clark:

THE ROAD TO NALIN
DESOLATION DREAMTIME
AN IMMACULATE CONCEPTION
*ANDREA
*AUSTRALIAN ADVENTURERS
*MOTHERHOOD

with **Iain Finlay**

GOOD MORNING HANOI
THE SILK TRAIN
*AFRICA OVERLAND
*SOUTH AMERICA OVERLAND
*ACROSS THE SOUTH PACIFIC

Titles marked with an asterisk were originally
published under Trish's previous name,
Trish Sheppard.

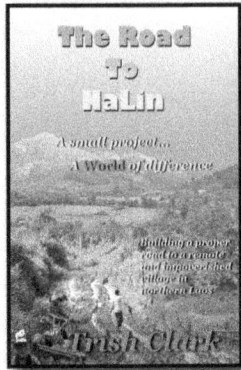

THE ROAD TO NALIN
A Small Project...
A World of Difference
Trish Clark

An inspirational story of how an older Australian couple, Trish Clark and Iain Finlay, both journalists in their seventies, built a decent road to a remote and impoverished village in northern Laos.

While visiting the home village of a young waiter who they were helping with his English skills, they were shocked by the almost total lack of facilities; no running water, no electricity at the time, a less than basic sewage system, no medical facilities and an under-resourced primary school. But worst of all, their only access to the outside world...a shocking track that turned into an almost impassabe knee-deep quagmire every rainy season.

So Trish and Iain decided to try to tackle something they knew absolutely nothing about. They set out to build a proper road to the village of NaLin.

(Available now in hard copy and eBook formats)

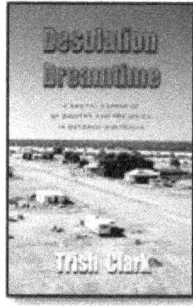

DESOLATION DREAMTIME
A Brutal Exposé of Bigotry and Prejudice in Outback Australia
Trish Clark

Causing a storm of controversy on first publication, under the title *Children of Blindness*, this is a powerful drama set in the small, fictional, but archetypal outback country town of Woongarra, depicts with stunning force, the violent interaction of a small group of people; black and white, over a period of little more than a week, in which three of them die.

Based on actual events at the time, this searing novel opens with Dougo Foster returning from six months in prison to find his children taken into care because of gross neglect by his drunken, pregnant wife, Flo. His attempts to get them back are the central thread along which the story unfolds, revealing layer upon layer of alcohol-fuelled degradation, violence and hopelessness for the indigenous community, amidst virtual total disapprobation and contempt from most of the white residents of the town. But fortunately not all.

And then there's the law; the compassionate cop, in contrast to his red-neck colleague, who regards all aborigines as hopeless bloody boongs. There is, however, little either can do when a series of events combine to tip the teetering township over the edge, into a night of unremitting horror.

(Available now in hard copy and eBook formats)

AN IMMACULATE CONCEPTION
Trish Clark

'...just when you thought it was safe
to
get on
with your own life.'

Cathy Connolly is revelling in the newfound joys of being Sam's grandmother. At work she is Ms. Catherine Stuart, a high-powered, senior executive in the Education Department. She's in good health, her husband Steve, is a successful architect, she has a happy daughter, a settled son and daughter-in-law, an erratic but charmingly likable brother and a distant, but well-loved mother.

Suddenly, within the space of less than two weeks, her life plunges into disarray. A colleague at work is trying to push her out of her job, Steve wants to take off in a 4-wheel drive for the Kimberleys, her daughter has given her boyfriend the boot, her brother wants to leave his wife and two daughters for a woman twenty-five years younger, and her son is donating his sperm to a lesbian couple. But, worst of all, Cathy finds she has cervical cancer.

'Life has taken a sudden lurch,' her voice was tremulous. 'Last week it all seemed so simple and straightforward. I feel as though I have stepped off into the deep end.'

'Just keep treading water and ring your Mum.' Steve told her.'

A fascinating and witty slice of modern Australian life, An Immaculate Conception highlights the dramatically changing standards, morals, and attitudes, not only of the cool, modish inhabitants of Sydney's eastern beach suburbs, where it is set, but of the whole country.

(Available now in hard copy and eBook formats)

A N D R E A
Trish Clark

Ahead of the kiss and tell pack by several decades *Andrea* was a close intimate of European royalty and silent-screen Hollywood stars as well as Australian politicians and socialites. She also spent four character-building years in a Japanese prisoner of war camp.

At the time of its publication her no-holds-barred biography caused a legal flurry at the highest levels. Despite demands for its publication to be banned, it has gone on to become an established social history of a time when live radio was the power domain and Andrea was its Queen. 'He was up me like a rat up a rope,' is just one of her earthy comments about an Australian Prime Minister.

Now, with all her personal papers stored in their own archive at the Library of NSW its time to re-read her story and be amazed how little has changed when it comes to Sex, Money and Politics.

(Digital version in production)

M O T H E R H O O D
Trish Clark

Fifteen women living through the various stages of motherhood from pregnancy to the anticipation of an empty nest, reveal their innermost desires and fears. While dealing with the unexpected blows of early widowhood, an offspring's physical incapacity, or even a child's death from drug addiction, they unveil the determination and courage that is at the core of their chosen lifelong role.

Strung along the thread of the author's own experiences their survival mantra, at a time when the choice for motherhood is no longer a natural given, is the feeling that there is only one thing worse than having children and that is not having them.

(Digital version in production)

AUSTRALIAN ADVENTURERS
Trish Clark

What drives a person to purposely place themselves beyond the comfortable, safe borders of the known; to push on further, to the risky edge and perhaps even over it?

Is there some intangible physic payment for placing yourself in physical jeopardy? Is that reward so addictive that it cannot be resisted as it grows to be a compulsion beyond family, friends, financial reward, even life itself.

Twenty *Australian Adventurers,* of all ages, share the passion that drives them to film sharks in the wild, climb Everest or become Australia's first aviatrix. To solo sail or to helicopter solo around the world. To voyage alone in the Antarctic or to recreate the 4000-kilometer open boat voyage of the Bounty mutineers. To be determined to hold the world hang gliding records for both height and distance at the same time, or to be the first to canoe right around the Australian continent. To put grandmotherhood on hold in order to become a backpacker, or to join the wartime resistance. Stories about those who dare ...to delight and challenge those who stay at home.

(Digital version in production)

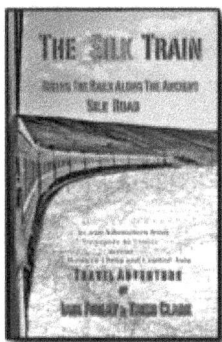

THE SILK TRAIN
Iain Finlay & Trish Clark

EXCELLENCE
e-Lit Awards

The Silk Train is award–winning travel adventure with a geo-political backbone. Veteran journalists Iain Finlay and Trish Clark set out to travel 21,000 kilometres from Singapore to Venice, by hopping on and off trains up through South East Asia, across China, Central Asia, the Caucasus, Turkey and the Balkans. Much of their route covers territory along which the ancient Silk Road trails wound their way over the past two thousand years. They planned to use rail lines that form part of an embryonic, UN-backed Trans-Asian Railway network, that will eventually create unbroken freight and passenger corridors all the way from China's far-eastern seaboard, to Europe.

While visiting some of the great historic sites of China and Central Asia, among them: Xi'an, Dunhaung, Samarkand and Bukhara, they also become aware of the changing dynamics of Big-Power politics across the vast Central Asian steppes, once the stamping grounds of Genghis Khan and Tamerlane, which now include the newly independent countries of Kazakhstan, Kyrgyzstan and Uzbekistan. They very quickly realise that, by far the most important items of trade along the modern equivalents of the Silk Road, are now oil and natural gas. Oil is the new silk. It is the new trans-national currency of the Silk Road, with China and its voracious, seemingly insatiable appetite for energy, emerging as the most significant factor in the political and economic arena of Central and South East Asia.

Further west, Russia's increased pressure on the Caucasus, particularly Georgia, is just another indication of how vital the world's dwindling energy resources are and will remain for most of the twenty-first century. By journey's end, in Venice, they realise they have travelled a very different Silk Road than that of Marco Polo.

(Illustrated hard copy version available now)

GOOD MORNING HANOI
Iain Finlay & Trish Clark

When Iain Finlay and Trish Clark arrive in Hanoi on a one-year work assignment for the English language service of the communist government-run radio network, they can hardly foresee the intense and exceptional experiences that await them. Coming to Vietnam for an Australian aid agency, their intended role is to coach and instruct, or at least to share their knowledge, with a small group of young reporters. But they find that they learn more than they teach.

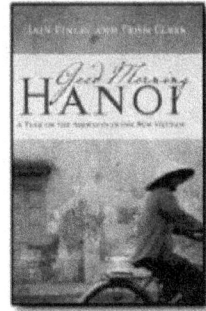

As friendships with their colleagues grow, Iain and Trish are involved in developing and presenting a daily radio program - the first run by Westerners on a regular basis - and they become immersed in the stimulating life of one of Asia's most enchanting cities. In the process, they gain fascinating insights into Vietnamese society and culture, as well as a greater understanding and respect for the new Vietnam.

Good Morning Hanoi also illuminates the lives of a group of people dwelling in crowded conditions around a small courtyard in central Hanoi where Iain and Trish find a house to rent, and who become like an extended family living in the heart of the city.

In Good Morning Hanoi, Iain and Trish, two of the founders and producers of the international television program Beyond 2000, return to a country from which they had reported during the Vietnam War. They find an extraordinarily friendly people whose resilience and irrepressible good nature enable them to put the past behind them and move into the future with confidence.

(Illustrated hard copy version available now)

328

By Iain Finlay & Trish Clark
THREE INCREDIBLE ADVENTURES:

Africa Overland
South America Overland
Across the South Pacific

You'd love to travel to remote and exotic places but...you have kids. So? Why let that stop you? You're worried about their education...think you should wait. Don't!

Iain and Trish didn't. They made three big journeys through some of the toughest territories in Africa, North and South America and the South Pacific with their two young children. Using public transport; buses, trains, trucks, trading vessls, sometimes hitching, each of them shouldering their own backpack, they spent months at a time on the road.

Spread over period of just on four years, their travels took them first from Capetown to Cairo. Eighteen months later they journeyed overland from Canada to Tierra del Fuego, at the bottom tip of South America and within another year and a half, they island hopped across the South Pacific from Chile to Australia.

Not only did they survive to write these three books, which also look at the history, politics and way of life of the countries through which they traveled, but, with the passing of the years they know their travel adventures truly sealed an on-going adult friendship with their children.

(Read on

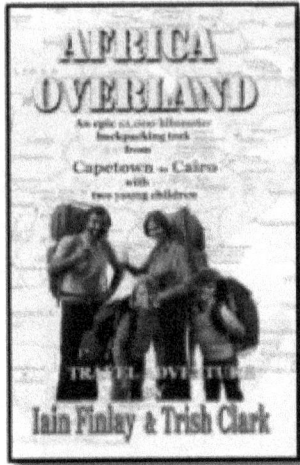

AFRICA OVERLAND
Iain Finlay & Trish Clark

Capetown to Cairo! A magical phrase...the journey of a lifetime. Around 12,000 kilometers, nine countries, four months on the road with nothing booked or arranged in advance. With their two children; a son aged eight and daughter nine, carrying their own back-packs and often sleeping in rough circumstances (like in the back of a truck laden with copper ingots), Iain, Trish and the kids get to see: Kruger National Park, Victoria Falls and travel on the TanZam railway. They experience the vast herds of game in Serengetti, Lake Manyara,Ngorongoro Crater and Amboseli, go to the source of the Blue Nile in Ethiopia, travel on 'Kitchener's Railway' across the Nubian Desert from Khartoum to Wadi Halfa, Aswan and the great temples of the Nile Valley... all the way down to Cairo and the Pyramids.

(Illustrated digital version in production)

SOUTH AMERICA OVERLAND
by Iain Finlay & Trish Clark

This incredible journey includes much more than just South America. It starts in Canada as Iain, Trish, their ten-year-old son and daughter, aged eleven, set out in a blizzard that covers most of the US, to deliver a car cross-country to San Diego. Then they travel by train and bus through Mexico, Belize, Guatamala, El Salvador, Honduras, Nicaragua and Costa Rica to Panama. Along the way they visit the great Aztec and Mayan temples of Tenochtitlan, Palenque, Tikal and many others.

Then on to Ecuador and Peru, where they puzzle over the mysterious lines in the Nazca Desert and visit the fabled Lost City of the Incas at Machu Picchu. Across the Andes, on the Amazon headwaters, at Pucallpa and down-river, they find barges, ferryboats and a trading boat for a 3,000-kilometer, month-long journey down the Amazon to Iquitos and Manaus.

On through the Matto Grosso to Bazilia, Rio and Sao Paulo, Iguasu Falls, Montevideo and Buenos Aires, before hitching for much of the way south through Patagonia to the amazing glaciers of southern Argentina, the Magellan Straits and Tierra del Fuego. Here they reach the southernmost city in the world, Ushuaia,   Six months, 17 countries, 23,000 kilometers:

(Illustrated digital version in production)

ACROSS THE SOUTH PACIFIC
by Iain Finlay & Trish Clark

Leaving Santiago, Chile after a frightening night of earth tremors, Iain, Trish and their two children, now 12 and 13 years old, fly to Easter Island, where, using their own tents, they camp out in remote corners of the island as they explore the huge, enigmatic stone monoliths. From there, its Tahiti and the stunning beauty of Bora Bora, Morea and the unbelievable Tuamotu atolls.

In the Cook Islands they board a copra trading vessel for a journey through the island chain; Aitutaki, Rakahanga and Manihiki. When it breaks down, mid-ocean, they go overboard with the crew to swim in water 3,000 metres deep. American and Western Samoa are next, in the midst of a typhoon.

Then the pleasures and beauty of Tonga, the Fiji Islands, Vanuatu and New Caledonia, before finally returning to their home in Australia.

(Illustrated digital version in production)

Highadventurepublishing.com
and
Highadventureproductions.com
are part of
High Adventure Productions
PO Box 111
Tumbulgum, NSW 2490
email: iaintrish@mac.com
AUSTRALIA

www.ingramcontent.com/pod-product-compliance
Lightning Source LLC
Chambersburg PA
CBHW022329280326
41934CB00006B/581